101+

THINGS TO DO WITH

glitter

Momtaz Begum-Hossain

Vivays Publishing

Published by Vivays Publishing Ltd
www.vivays-publishing.com

Copyright © 2012 Momtaz Begum-Hossain

A catalogue record for this book is available from
the British Library

ISBN 978-1-908126-23-8

Publishing Director: Lee Ripley
Design: Struktur Design
Printed in China

CONTENTS

GLITTER: A LOVE AFFAIR

Whether you spot it in a dew drop resting on a blade of grass, are enchanted by the shimmering beams illuminating the disco walls around you, or you just like that embossed font on your Christmas card; there is no denying that glitter is all around us. From the great outdoors to fashion, paving slabs to cupcakes, these twinkling specks of loveliness can transform the ordinary into a thing of extreme beauty. Glitter has many qualities and not just adding dazzle to craft projects. It has the power to evoke mood – most commonly putting you in a good one! Glitter possesses magical properties that inspire our inner child, making us feel excited, uplifted and happy. The vibrancy of the shades combined with their changing hues as they glisten in the light is a miracle of nature, even though glitter itself is human-made.

I cannot remember a time when glitter was not in my life. At school, like every other classmate, I was fascinated at how just a dab of sparkle could transform my art. When I was 12 years old, my sister worked in a chemist and one day she came home and told me they had started selling 'Glitter Bug Gel', an iridescent body glitter. I had never seen anything like it and I took several trips to the store to stare at it on the shelf and the brilliance of the particles, glimmering under the shop lights. I used to imagine what it would be like to actually wear it, until eventually I got to try a tester and realised this was it: I had well and truly fallen in love. In the years that followed, glitter cosmetics, clothing, products and crafting glitter were available in abundance, in every size, shape and shade imaginable. Suddenly the possibilities were endless...anything could sparkle. In an instant, a sprinkling of light-reflecting particles had the power to change everything.

Despite its allure and irresistibility, glitter is commonly misunderstood. Some people think it is just for children, is only seasonal and that it

Janine Basil

Through the ages   Glitter has been a part of society since time began.

40,000 to 200 B.C.: Ancient glamour
Civilisations throughout history (Egyptian, Chinese, Greek, Roman) were attracted to shiny things and used shimmering mica flakes in their wall paintings.

1930s: The birth of consumer glitter
Henry Ruschmann of Bernardsville, New Jersey is officially regarded as the father of glitter. He invented what we know as glitter today, turning large quantities of plastic into tiny glittering particles. He set up one of the world's biggest manufacturers of glitter, Meadowbrook Inventions.

1960s: Beautifying shimmer
Shimmering powders, lipsticks and eyeshadows became easily accessible to the consumer when major brands such as Revlon, Estée Lauder, Elizabeth Arden, and Helena Rubinstein began selling glittery products that anyone could incorporate into their beauty routine.

1970s: Pop personas
David Bowie pioneered cosmetic glitter when he appeared as his androgynous alter ego Ziggy Stardust with a glittery lightning bolt painted across his face by make-up artist Pierre La Roche.

is too messy to use. None of this is true! (Ok... maybe the messy part is, but that is part of the charm.) Glitter has infinite uses, it is even used by forensics to track down criminals! This book aims to equip you with ideas and inspiration for how you can incorporate the sparkly stuff into your own life. There are over 100 project ideas showing contemporary uses of glitter that split into four sections: interiors, gifts, fashion and papercrafts. Over 150 types of glitter have been used in the projects and there are lots of innovative techniques to try with hints and tips along the way.

Keep the book to hand and flick through it whenever you need some creative motivation. You can follow the instructions for how to make each project, adapt them to your tastes or even combine ideas to come up with something truly unique. There are no rights or wrongs in making these projects- and certainly none in how you use glitter. The only restriction is your imagination.

Bridal mendi by Joshiv Beauty International.
Photographer Alexandre Pichon for Asiana Wedding magazine

1980s: Rock on
Rock bands followed suit with acts like Mötley Crüe and Poison mixing glitter into their huge hairdos adding extra stage presence. Eager young fans copied.

1990s: Sparkle epidemic
Glittery products became the norm and you no longer needed to buy loose glitter to get the effect you wanted. Glitter pens, paints, adhesives and materials were easily available on the high street.

2000s: Limited editions
The marketing world recognised the potential to capitalise on glitter by launching desirable products that stylish consumers could not wait to get their hands on, such as Gold Flakes Supreme Vodka containing 24 carat gold flakes, and Jean Paul Gaultier's Fragile fragrance contained in a glittering snow globe.

Present: A craft revolution
Glitter is no longer seen as something that is only for children. It has become a highly respected material in the crafting scene and makers everywhere are rediscovering the fun of working with it!

Future: It sparkles!
New brands and types of glitter continue to emerge, infiltrating into every aspect of society, making the world a happier place.

GLITTER IN CONTEMPORARY CULTURE

Bridalwear by Ekta Solanki
Photographer Alexandre Pichon for Asiana Wedding magazine

THE WORLD IS
A SCARY PLACE
BUT I HAVE ARMBANDS

Art: Glass Cathedrals
by Lisa Swerling
I like the way a single sparkle that
catches your eye can suggest the
existence of a whole other world.
I like the way glitter escapes into
cracks in my floorboards and is
never seen again, but may be invisibly
bolstering the foundations of my
house. My Glass Cathedrals works
are art boxes that contain tiny
universes, and make small statements
about life. Adding glitter to the
design instantly transforms the
spaces from the mundane,
into the magical.
(www.glasscathedrals.com)

Dazzling fireworks

Glistening disco ball

Pop icon Lady Gaga

Food: Wedding Cake
by Dan Amin
The invention of edible glitter has revolutionised the dessert industry with shimmering toppings making an appearance on biscuits, confectionary and cupcakes. For wedding cakes I love creating intricate patterns by applying edible glitter with stencils, then accessorising with details like glittery props. It beats having plain white icing!
(www.exclusivecakes4u.co.uk)

Fashion: Fascinators by Janine Basil
My style of hatmaking is about creating something that's fun, with a hint of burlesque, and a touch of geek. Glitter evokes nostalgia. We all recall making glittery pictures when we were young but now I'm grown up, I still love how it sparkles. I used to only use rhinestones in my work, until I rediscovered glitter!
(www.janinebasil.com)

Boot Seventeen Starry Eyes make-up advert from 1975

Twinkling stars in the milky way

A spangly carnival costume

ALL THAT GLITTERS...

We know we love it and we know it sparkles; but what exactly is glitter and how is it made? The mystery is about to be revealed...

Glitter is entirely human-made and starts off as one of several raw materials such as polyester (plastic), aluminum (metal) or a mixture of the two. These are melted into rolls of foil that are coated in metallic, neon and iridescent shades. When they hit light, they reflect a spectrum of colours, and this is what gives glitter its sparkle. Another secret is that the particles do not lie flat, so when light shines on them, the subtle angles make different colours appear.

Although it may look like they are crushed into tiny particles to become glitter, in actual fact, they are all individually cut into small pieces. To minimise waste, each speck is cut into a shape that fits together like hexagons, squares and rectangles.

Industrial glitter production

RJA Plastics, in Germany, is Europe's biggest glitter manufacturer and is run by the Coburn family. As well as creating 84 shades and 12 sizes of glitter, they design and sell glitter-making machines. The company specialises in manufacturing polyester, aluminium and cosmetic glitters, yet whatever type they are making, the process is the same:

Stage 1:
Film production

The film itself starts off as small particles of metal or plastic that are melted. A film producer then extrudes the film from the melted particles into a thin film, then metalises it. So interestingly it begins life as a small particle, turns into a long thin film and then goes back to being even smaller particles.

Stage 2:
Colour development and film coating

There is a lot of chemistry that goes into making glitter! It starts with a team of chemists working in a laboratory undertaking important tests like checking the chemical resistance and safety of the colourants that will be used to coat the glitter film. When a new colour is created it must be able to withstand numerous tests. For cosmetic glitter there are stringent guidelines to ensure all the colourants are health and safety approved for use on the body. The colorants that are created in the laboratory are then applied to the film, using a special coating and printing technique that results in colourful rolls of foil.

Stage 3:
Loading the machine

The freshly printed films are then brought to the cutting and screening room where they are placed on a glitter-cutting machine. The film is fed into the machine where a stationary knife and rotary knife are set up to make the shape of the glitter particle; either a hexagon, square or rectangle.

Stage 4:
Cutting and quality control

Once the cutting starts, a sample of freshly cut glitter is viewed under a microscope to ensure it is the perfect shape and if all the dimensions are correct the process continues. Engineers keep an eye over the process to ensure the entire batch is up to standard. They are also responsible for general maintenance and fixing the machines.

Stage 5:
Screening and sifting

The cut glitter accumulates and is taken to a screening area where it is screened according to its particle size, sifting out any larger or smaller pieces that may have sneaked in.

Stage 6:
Packaging and shipping

The glitter is then packaged and shipped to the customer, wherever they may be in the world. As for how it's used? There are over 101 ideas in this very book!

Images by RJA Plastics GmbH

9

TYPES OF GLITTER

Introducing the family... When it comes to choosing what type of glitter to use in a project, the options are endless. Take your pick from these varieties:

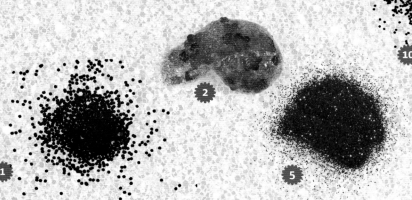

1 Black glitter
Many types of glitter are available in black, but they vary in their sheen. Some add texture rather than sparkle.

2 Confetti
Made up of small sequin shapes – can be loose or contained within glitter glue.

3 Cosmetic
These are tiny particles that have a magical twinkle and are used in make-up, face paint and beauty products.

4 Edible
Two types are available; a coarse grain that looks like a satin salt crystal, and fine grains that leave a shimmer when you sprinkle them on food. Both are available in a wide range of colours and neither have a taste.

5 Fine
Glitter that consists of small particles used for creating an opaque coverage. It is perfect for papercrafting projects.

6 Flock
A powder with glittery particles that can be used to create a 3D flocking effect.

7 Glass
The most expensive type of glitter, it captures a high quality diamond-like shine creating a mirror effect. It is cut from glass film so each shard differs in shape though it is available in 'sizes' so you can buy large or small glass glitter. The particles may be sharp so it should be handled with gloves and is only suitable for adult use.

8 Glue
Available in tubes and pens there are two varieties with different uses. The first is coloured or clear with particles suspended in it and is ideal for children's artwork. The second type is a high-density glue that looks more like liquid glitter. It has a vast number of uses, is available in infinite colours and is the quickest and easiest way to use glitter in almost any project.

9 Hexagonal
When you look closely you will see that each grain is hexagonal in shape. The particles are larger than 'standard' glitter so they are good for when you want your crafting to really have impact.

10 Holographic
These particles have a holographic effect when they catch the light creating a full spectrum of reflective colours. The glitter itself is available in different shades.

11 Leaf/flakes
A large coarsely cut glitter that looks almost like confetti. Good for using sparingly to appreciate each speck.

12 Mica
Not commonly used for crafting, mica is a natural mineral that has glittering properties. It is used in the luxury beauty industry for products that give your skin a healthy sheen and can also be bought as 'mica flakes', which are small gold fragments that are used by artists.

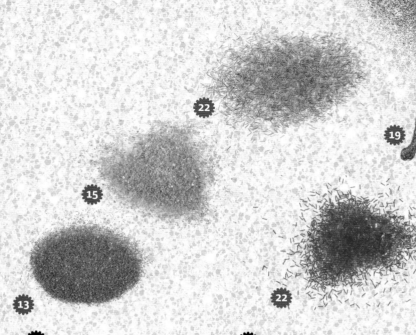
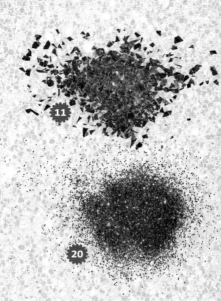

13 Metallic
Colours have a dull metal tone and work well in vintage crafting.

14 Microfine
This variety is so small it has a powdery and fairy dust-like quality. Its spectacular shimmery finish looks like a sheet of shininess.

15 Neon
This refers to the colour – neon glitters are extremely bright!

16 Pearlescent glitter
Has a satiny, opaque consistency creating a natural shimmer.

17 Pens
Use these to write greetings cards and add fine details. The inks are glittery and pens are available in different thicknesses.

18 Snow
A soft white glittery grain that is used as faux snow, making it perfect for winter crafting.

19 Spray on
Just like spray paint in a can, you can permanently spray glitter straight onto a surface, creating either light or full coverage depending on how much you use.

20 Standard
The classic glitter associated with children's crafting. It is usually available in the traditional shades of gold, silver, blue, red and green and is reflective rather than intensely coloured.

21 Superfine/ultrafine
Is even finer than microfine, you can barely see the specks. Commonly used in jewellery making.

22 Tinsel
A long grain that is light and creates a fluffy look. It also has a tonal sheen thanks to its feathery texture.

23 Transparent
Some white glitters are transparent and look like plastic particles adding a subtle shimmer while allowing the surface colour underneath to come through.

24 Varnish
Professional varnish sold in hardware shops. It can be used to embellish your interiors such as creating a glittering door or wall.

GLITTER SOS:
Everything you need to know about the sparkly stuff

There are no rules for how to use glitter but you might find these suggestions useful.

Applying glitter

Tempting as it may be, do not pour glitter straight onto glue, directly from a large container. Decant it onto something more manageable, like a teaspoon. Some glitter comes in plastic tubes that have pouring holes, which is really good for applying to small areas for an even control, allowing you to sprinkle what you need. Or you can make your own. Use a bottle that has a fine nozzle like an empty hair dye container, fill it with glitter then apply to your design. You can change the flow by cutting the opening; a bigger hole means more glitter will come out.

Saving glitter

After every project, excess glitter should be collected and returned to its original container to be used again. You will be surprised at how little you end up using per project. Sometimes it feels like you have used half a jar, yet when you pour it back barely a dent has been made! Often glitter can get trapped in the tiny crevices of your craft item where no glue has been applied. You can remove it with a dry brush. The easiest way to pour glitter back into a container is on a piece of paper. Fold it in half and let the glitter fall into the crease. The stronger the crease, the easier it will be to pour your glitter back.

It is not always possible to save all of it. Once air gets inside a pot, it can take up room and all of a sudden, your glitter no longer fits. Keep a separate empty container to collect your spare and scrap glitters, to create your own special 'rainbow mix', unlike any other shade in existence.

Tidying glitter up

Glitter will travel. It may end up between your nails, trapped in a rug, clinging to your clothes, get inside books, land in your sink, and even sparkle on your face; but that is part of the fun! Craft glitters are non-toxic so they are safe for use by anyone though your pet probably does not want to end up looking like a disco ball, in which case it is essential that you keep your glitter tidied up. All of these things will help:

✸ Wear an apron to protect your clothes
✸ Keep a card rectangle to scrape up loose glitter
✸ Use an old toothbrush to 'brush up' glitter
✸ If you are working on your lap, place a tray underneath you so any falling glitter will land in one place
✸ Double cover your work surfaces. Don't just work on a tablecloth; place another one underneath for extra protection.
✸ Lay paper down on the floor beneath where you are working if you think it is going to get messy, especially if there are children taking part.

Blending your own glitter:

Instead of using glitters bought straight from a shop, it's fun to mix different shades together to make your own colours, just as you would with paint. Ultrafine glitter works best. Pick two to three colours that complement each other and perhaps have a theme to them; purple, blue and green would be a great peacock shade. Avoid mixing textures together as fine glitter will loose its impact if blended with thicker grades and likewise, pale pastel colours can get lost when used with really striking shades. Add a teaspoon of one colour into a container, then add your second colour and stir together. Add the third colour, or if you are just using two, add a bit more of each shade, one teaspoon at a time until you get the quantity you need. Name the shade and add a label.

Drying glitter

It is better not to leave crafts to dry on newspaper, as you may end up with 'newsprint' on your design. Instead, place them on a non-stick surface, like greaseproof paper/baking parchment. Sometimes it is tricky to handle an object because you have glued the ends and cannot pick it up. For small items, you can stand them up to dry by attaching a cocktail stick with a sticky re-usable putty, but for most things you will need to do one side, wait for it to dry, and then turn it over.

Removing glitter from clothes

Just in case glitter does land on your clothes and you are not keen on the new sparkly look, fear not, it can be removed. All you need is an ordinary aerosol hairspray. Spray it directly onto the glittery patch, then wait for it to dry and harden. When you place your garment in the washing machine, the detergent will try its best to shift the hairspray, taking the glitter with it. If you have been using PVA glue and glitter, and it gets on your clothes, you can pick it off when it hardens, just as PVA peels away from your skin when it dries.

Where to store glitter:

Never store glitter in a container without a lid; if it spills it will be tricky to rescue! Glitter looks best in glass jars, left on a windowsill where the specks can capture the sunrays, making them look their sparkly best. Try:

* Empty spice jars
* Salt and pepper towers
* Jam jars and food jars
* Small plastic pots
* Labelled matchboxes
* Empty cosmetic tins

Making glitter last

Glitter is prone to flaking off. You can prevent this by adding a protective layer of adhesive or gloss. Each project in the book will recommend how you can do this. The general way is to either topcoat your project with a protective glue or varnish, like spraying on an adhesive. With so many types of craft adhesives on the market, it is important you use the right one for your project. While you can swap brands and colours of glitter to your taste, try and use the suggested glues to get the best results.

Homemade glitter:

If you fancy making a glitter that is totally unique, try making your own using these DIY techniques:

Salt glitter

Preheat an oven to 170°C/340°F. Place salt (either table or sea salt) into a small bowl. Measure as much as you want to make. Add a drop of food colouring and mix well into the salt so it covers it evenly without becoming clumpy. Spread the mixture onto a baking sheet in one layer and bake in the oven on a tray for 10 minutes. Separate any lumps that may have formed with a fork. When cool, transfer the mixture into a storage container. For added sparkle spray the grains with a little coating of glitter spray.

Sand glitter

Choose a fine grain of sand that has a natural sparkle to it. Have a look for it, next time you are visiting the coast. Not all seasides have sparkly sand, but pebbly beaches often have it right at the shoreline. Place a small amount into a bowl and gradually mix in a few drops of pen ink or food dye. Mix thoroughly and ensure the grains stay separated. Store in a container until needed for crafting.

A-Z OF CRAFTING INSPIRATION

Throughout the book you will see suggestions for how to decorate objects with glitter, but you don't need to find the exact item to have a go at the project. Crafting is about being creative with what you have at home or can get hold of easily. You certainly don't need to spend lots of money. There are so many places you can go to find items that can be customised or to get the materials you need to make projects from scratch. These places are also great inspirational haunts where you can jot down ideas, draw sketches or take photographs of things you like.

A

Art & craft markets
Handmade items you would like to have a go at making.

Antique shops
One-of-a-kind ornaments you have never seen before.

Auctions
Furniture that will look great in your home.

B

Book fairs
Old craft books for project ideas.

Bookshops
The latest craft books to stay ahead of crafting trends.

C

Car boot sales
Records, CDs and DVDs.

Charity shops
Cutlery and crockery.

Craft stores
New crafting materials and techniques.

D

Department stores
Designer gifts and homeware.

Dreams
Places you saw and people you met.

E

Ethnic shops
Printed fabrics.

F

Friends
Unwanted belongings.

Films:
Costumes and locations.

Flea markets
Broken objects that can be fixed.

G

Galleries
Exhibitions that interest you.

H

Haberdasheries
Pretty trimmings and fabric remnants.

Hardware shops
Tools to help make your crafts.

Holidays
Ethnic fabrics and jewellery.

I

Internet
Specialist craft materials.

J
Jumble sale
Bric-a-brac.

K
Kitsch stores
Colourful trinkets and knick-knacks.

L
Library
Books and magazines.

M
Magazines
Imagery and photoshoots.

Music videos
Fashion trends.

N
Nightlife
Interiors of nightclubs and clubwear.

O
Open houses
Home studios and workspaces.

P
Pound shops
Containers to store your craft materials.

Q
Quirky people
Unusually dressed people, note down colour and outfit combinations.

R
Relatives
'Hand-me-downs' and family heirlooms.

S
Sales
Clothing that can be customised.

School fêtes
Toys and children's items.

Scrapyards
Metal and plastic objects and signs.

Supermarkets
Special offers and reductions.

T
Travelling
Take in the scenery wherever you are.

U
Unwanted junk
Abandoned furniture on the street.

V
Village fairs
Traditional crafts and games.

Vintage fairs
Fashion and interiors fabrics.

W
Work colleagues
Spare stationery.

X
Xmas markets
Seasonal gifts and decorations.

Y
Yard sales
Technology.

Z
Zoo
Animals!

CAPTURING INSPIRATION

Every time you see something you like, make a note of it. Draw, sketch, photograph or write a description of it so that next time you need creative inspiration you have a stash of ideas to turn to. Whether it is colour combinations, fabric choice, or graphic shapes that appeal to you, these visual and written references will give your crafts a designer edge.

Sketchbook

Keep all your inspirations and samples inside a book. There are no rules for how your sketchbook should look. Here are some ideas for what you could include…

Collages

Photographs

Drawings

Wrapping paper

Fashion photography

Food packaging

Postcards

Illustrations, Words, Fonts

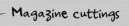
Magazine cuttings

Swatches

Business cards

Flower Power

Stickers
Gallery brochures
Greeting cards
Leaflets
Pamphlets

Flyers

Fabrics

Mood boards

Mood boards are a collection of visuals you like based around one idea that are stuck down onto large pieces of card or paper that you can hang up in your workspace for immediate inspiration.

Noticeboard

This is a good way to display ideas for current projects. When they are complete you can take them down and pin up inspirations for the next one.

Virtual images

If you are not a fan of cutting and sticking or do not have the time or space for it, you can keep an online record of things you like. Pinterest (www.pinterest.com) is a website that allows you to 'pin' images onto virtual pinboards that you can share with others. You can follow users and 're-pin' their suggestions. Or use an image-based blog like Tumblr (www.tumblr.com) to post pictures you like and store your photographs on sites like Flickr (www.flickr.com) so you can view your inspirations when you are on the move.

CRAFT STASH: BASIC MATERIALS

Every crafter should have one! It contains the basic materials you need to make the projects in this book. Some of them are probably already in your collection and others are worth buying because they can be used again. I keep most of my stash inside a huge toolbox, the type handymen like to fill with nails and screwdrivers. I also have a shelf at home for paints and glues, a drawer for papers and a gigantic box full of fabrics.

Paper
A4 (8 ½ x 11 in) sized paper is good for folding in half and returning glitter into its jar. Coloured paper is needed for projects.

Brushes (different sizes)
These are the best way to apply glue, as well as to paint surfaces. Fine brushes are essential for detail and big brushes for large areas.

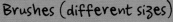

Stationery

Card
Colouring pencils
Eraser
Marker pens
Metal ruler
Pair of compasses
Pencils
Pens
Sharpener
Tracing paper

Acrylic paints

Own a rainbow of colours as you never know what mood you will be in. Acrylic paints can be used on card and wood and give an opaque coverage. Keep a bottle of white for mixing shades and applying undercoats.

Glues and adhesives

The glue aisle at craft stores can be overwhelming as there are so many brands, but luckily they all have their uses, and for glitter crafting you will need several types:

3D foam pads
All purpose glue
Blu-Tack (or other repositionable gum)
Double-sided tape
Fabric glue
Glue gun (and glue sticks)
Masking tape (wide and thin)
Mod Podge (thick collage glue)
PVA (or other white craft glue)
Silicone
Spray adhesive
Strong glues (solvent free)
Superglue
Tacky glue
Velcro (hook and loop tape)

Fine tip applicator

A specially designed product that allows you to apply PVA glue in very fine lines (0.5mm) which you can then cover in glitter. Perfect for details.

Scissors

You will need sharp scissors to cut through fabric and a pair for general crafting that you do not mind getting sticky. Once you start cutting through double-sided tape you will understand why! It is also good to invest in a craft knife and mat.

Sewing kit

If you are a regular sewing fan you may already have a sewing machine. Occasional sewers should keep a needle, thread, pins, tape measure, iron and some iron-on fusible webbing in your stash.

CRAFT STASH: SPECIAL MATERIALS

Acrylic gems
For instant bling use gems, stones or crystals in your work. Some have adhesive backs and can be made permanent by using a Hot Fix Applicator.

Fabric
A very important part of your stash! Look out for unusual remnants and pretty prints or cut up old clothes.

Motifs/embellishments
Collect an assortment of materials like synthetic flowers and iron-on patches to add interesting details to your designs.

Sequins
Add even more shimmer to your 'makes' with a sprinkling of sequin

Beads
There are beads for every occasion! Build up a selection of assorted shapes, sizes and colours.

Buttons
Decorative buttons can be incorporated into all types of crafts from fashion to papercrafts.

Pompoms
These can be stitched through or glued on and bring a fun texture to collages.

Trimmings
Come in infinite variations from fluffy and embroidered to bobbled. They can instantly transform a project.

CRAFT STASH APRON

Glitter and glue are a messy combination so protect your clothes with an apron when you are crafting. Opt for a wipe clean fabric or a cotton that you can easily wash. Ensure it has a nice print – perhaps with your favourite animal on, and if possible, always have an apron with a pocket as they are very useful!

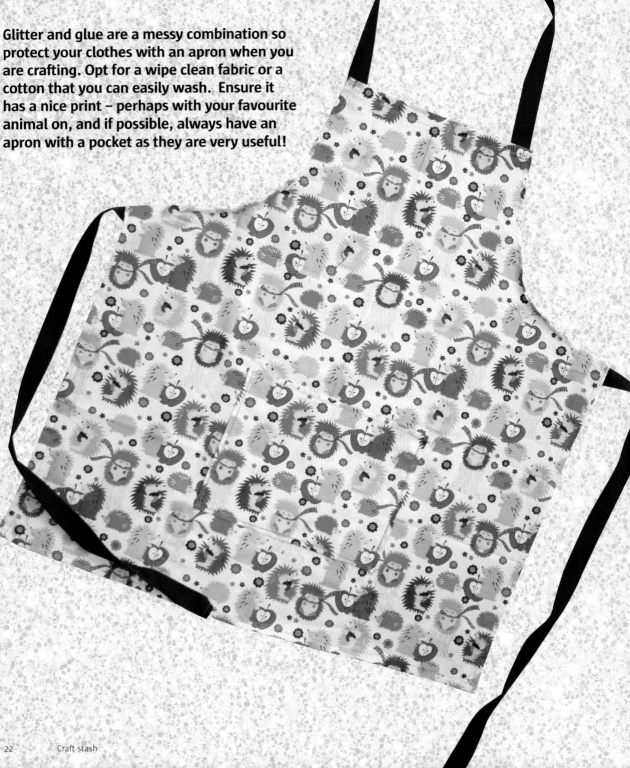

MASTER IT!
HOW TO MAKE
GLITTER FABRIC/GLITTER CARD/
GLITTER FOAM

CRAFT STASH:

* A piece of vinyl fabric, sheet of cardboard or funky foam/neoprene
* PVA glue
* Glitter of your choice
* Spray adhesive
* Paintbrush

MAKE IT

1. Cover your preferred material in a smooth layer of PVA glue, using the paintbrush. If the application is too thick it will run, creating lumps, resulting in an uneven coverage. On a large piece of fabric, it will be easier to do this a section at a time.

2. Sprinkle glitter along the whole surface or the section you are working on.

3. Use your fingers to flatten the glitter down and if there are gaps created, then add more glitter. Try not to use more glue, as it will create bumps.

4. Shake off the excess glitter onto paper and leave to dry.

5. To finish, spray on a coat of adhesive spray.

6. When the entire fabric, foam or card is dry, you can use it in your crafting.

MASTER IT! CONQUERING THE PROJECT TECHNIQUES

Whatever your experience of making things, there are endless craft techniques to enjoy. Some you may already do, or perhaps you have never heard of them? In these projects, as well as learning about glitter, you'll also be testing out and mastering techniques that will become part of your craft repertoire.

ANGELINA FIBRES

1 These are fine shimmery fibres that bond together in a process that requires an iron and greaseproof paper. Layer up individual fibres on the paper and 'trap' other materials inside like glitter or sequins.

2 Place a second sheet of paper on top and then iron over it on a medium setting.

3 After a few seconds the fibres will form a sheet of fabric. This can be cut up or joined to more fibres to create a longer piece. Any scrap or spare fibres can be bonded and used again. Always iron on the paper, not directly onto the fibres as they may damage your iron.

APPLIQUÉ

For this you cut motifs from fabric and affix them onto a second piece of fabric. You will need an iron and some iron-on fusible webbing. There are two types: a fabric version and a paper-backed variety that is much easier to work with. The paper-backed version has two sides; one is paper and the other has a layer of glue. Place your webbing, glue side down, onto the fabric you want to cut from, and iron over it using an even pressure on a medium heat. It will bond immediately.

1. Either draw a shape you want to cut out on the paper side, or turn it over and cut out your chosen fabric motif.

2. Peel off the paper to reveal a shiny surface.

3. Place it on your main fabric, shiny side down, and iron over it again so it sticks. To prolong its life, especially on garments, either outline with fabric tube paint or sew over the edges with a zigzag stitch on a sewing machine.

DRAWING

The best advice for drawing is to practise by doodling whenever you have a spare minute. Find a pencil or pen that you like working with and use it to sketch things you see. It does not matter if they are not in proportion or do not look right. Just keep trying! If you want a specific image, look for how other people have drawn it (the internet is good for this) as a guide. You can also trace copyright free images to use in your craft designs.

CLAY

The two clays here are air-dry that hardens naturally, and Fimo which hardens in a conventional oven. Start by breaking off a chunk and warming it between your palms to soften. To cut it into the shapes you require, roll it out with a small rolling pin onto a greaseproof paper surface. Air-dry clay can be shaped using cutters. For both, add any holes into the design before leaving to dry or bake. When using Fimo, clean the rolling pin and change the paper between colours, otherwise they may blend. For baking, follow the manufacturer's instructions. Fimo cooks on a low heat for 30 minutes. Small pieces will harden quicker. Do not leave longer than the recommended time as this can discolour the clay.

CUTTING

For cardmaking you will get a cleaner finish if you use a paper guillotine. Line your paper up with the blade and gently pull the rotary cutter along. The next best implement is a craft knife and mat. To use a knife, keep the blade flat, and gently pull it along, holding it up against a solid ruler. Do not hold the blade at an angle as it will not cut as well. For scissors you will need at least three types; one that is only used for fabric, another for cutting paper and a third that you don't mind getting sticky for cutting tapes and adhesive-backed papers.

MASTER IT!
CONQUERING THE
PROJECT TECHNIQUES

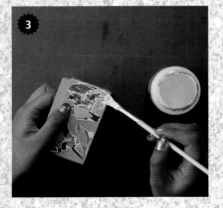

DECOUPAGE

The 2D method is a flat collage technique that preserves paper images. Start by cutting out pictures, text or motifs from paper (you can buy decoupage sheets) or use images from publications or wrapping paper.

1 Apply a white glue on the back of it (PVA or Mod Podge).

2 Smooth it onto the object you want to decorate.

3 To seal in the design apply a thin coat of clear varnish.

HEAT

Heat tools can adhere, melt, mould, emboss and even shrink things. There are three types in this book: hot glue guns, hot fix applicators and heat embossing guns.

✦ Hot glue guns work by heating and melting glue sticks to create a strong glue. You need to work fast as it cools very quickly.

✴ Hot Fix applicators permanently adhere Hot Fix gemstones (acrylic gems that have an adhesive back). They have a metal prodder that, once hot, fixes a gem to fabric, simply by holding it there for a few seconds.

✴ Heat embossing guns are like mini hairdryers and can be used for shrinking plastic. Draw a design on the plastic and place it in a baking tray. Direct your heat gun at it. The drawing will move around a lot at this point, follow it with your gun. When it has stopped shrinking use a flat block to flatten your drawing. Make any holes in the plastic before heating it. You can also shrink it in a conventional oven.

IMAGE TRANSFER

Transferring images used to be something you could only do at copy centres but now there is an easy method you can do at home as long as you have a printer. Lazertran is a product that allows you to transfer images onto to any surface including wood, glass, ceramics and fabric. Create an image digitally (upload a photograph or scan in a picture), and print it onto the correct type of Lazertran paper. Waterslide decal paper was used in the cufflinks project and allows images to be transferred to solid objects. Cut out the printed image, and place it in a bowl of water. The image will slide off leaving the backing paper behind. Smooth the image onto your object and it will stick on. For ceramics the transfers need to be heat fixed in a conventional oven and on other items the image can be varnished to seal it in place.

MASTER IT! CONQUERING THE PROJECT TECHNIQUES

SILIGUM

Siligum lets you create a re-usable mould. It is purchased in a kit that contains two colours of clay (blue and white).

1. You need to take equal quantities of each and roll them into a ball.

2. Ensure the two colours are evenly mixed together by using your hands so that the colours are evenly mixed together.

3. Roll it out (a few millimetres is sufficient) and coat the object you want to take a mould of. The mould sets in five minutes so you need to work quickly. It will come away from your object easily and will look like a rubber cast of it. If it has any holes, fill these with small bits of gum, otherwise your cast will not work. It can be used to mould plaster, resin and wax and be re-filled and re-used up to 50 times.

RESIN

Two-part epoxy resin consists of a hardener and crystal resin that can be purchased as a kit in craft shops. Resin is poured into moulds to make new objects and will suspend any items placed inside it. To find out how much resin you require you will need to measure your mould. Do this by filling it with water and then pour the water into a measuring jug to check. Whatever the measurement of the mould, you need to mix one part hardener with two parts resin.

When you combine the two, stir very gently or you will create bubbles that will set in the resin. Before pouring the mixture into a mould, the mould must be completely dry and greased all over with Vaseline or another petroleum jelly; this helps ease the object out. Pour the resin in slowly and leave it to set in a warm, dry place where it will be flat. Resin will set more quickly in warm places but generally you should wait 24 hours before de-moulding. Once it is removed, wash it thoroughly in cool water, pat dry and smooth off any rough edges or bumps with sand paper. As the resin and hardener are chemicals, work in a well ventilated area, wear plastic gloves and always cover your work surfaces, as once hardened, resin is extremely difficult to remove.

PAPERMAKING

The papermaking project in this book shows you how to recycle existing paper into new sheets. Take any paper and tear into strips. Place these into a blender with warm water. Close the lid and blend on high until a watery pulp is created. Add any additional materials like glitter or dried flowers. Make a screen by taping a piece of gauze onto a picture frame with the centre section and glass removed.

1 Press the pulp onto the gauze and spread it out.

2 Flip it onto a piece of felt to dry. The pulp will come away from the gauze as one sheet. If bits are left behind, scrape these off. Felt is a good drying surface as the pulp will not stick. Drying may take few days so be patient!

PAPIER-MÂCHÉ

This method allows you to make a paper cast of an object. To make a basic paste, mix spoonfuls of flour and water together in a ratio of four to one. Stir until it forms a runny paste. You can add more water if required. You also need to prepare strips of newspaper, by ripping or cutting them up. Do not make them too big or worry about making them an equal size. When you mould an object, rest it onto something so you can work without holding it. Wearing gloves, dip each piece of newspaper into the paste then smooth it onto the object, randomly. Build up two to three layers and leave to dry fully. This can take around 36 hours.

PAINTING

The trick to professional results is having good quality brushes. Before you start, cover all the work surfaces and use masking tape to seal off any part of the object that you do not want paint to land on. No matter how careful you are, paint has a tendency to drip when you least expect it; don't let this ruin your design! Always paint in one direction so that you can't see where strokes stop and start. On larger surfaces, try starting in the centre, and swirling your paint outwards. Many paints need more than one layer for full coverage. Wait until each layer is dry before applying the next and do it in a well-lit area so that you can see the coverage properly. Paintbrushes should be washed immediately after use. Oil paint can only be removed with white spirit. To clean, leave brushes to soak in a bowl. Do not use your hands to wash them or you may find they are stained for several days.

FASHION & ACCESSORIES

SHOE STOPPER

Dorothy from The Wizard of Oz owned the most iconic glittery fashion item in popular culture; her beautiful red shoes. She used them to get back home to Kansas, but if you click your heels while wearing your own pair, you never know what may happen...

MAKE IT:

1 Stick masking tape along the shoe edges, the bottom of the heel and the inside rims.

2 Paint your shoes red and allow to dry. The surface of your shoe will dictate which type of paint you use, acrylic paint will work for most surfaces or if it a fabric shoe use fabric paint.

3 Create a mixture of half Mod Podge and half glitter, and stir it together thoroughly.

4 Paint this mixture over the entire surface of the shoe. Apply it as evenly as possible. Do not create lumps as the shoe will dry unevenly. You will need to apply about three coats.

5 Mod Podge creates a protective shield against any glitter falling off so your glitter will stay on permanently, however it can make the sparkle look dull. To enhance its sheen, paint on a thin layer of PVA glue and sprinkle with an additional layer of glitter.

6 To complete Dorothy's shoes, use the template to make a bow from vinyl fabric. Glitter it up in the same way as you did the shoe (if it is red there is no need to paint it). Apply three coats of Mod Podge and glitter mix. Use the glue gun to affix these in the centre of the shoes.

CRAFT STASH:

* Pair of heeled shoes
* Paint (red - you need a type suitable for the surface of your shoe)
* PVA glue
* Glue gun
* Masking tape
* Paintbrush
* Mod Podge
* Scissors
* Clean pot
* Vinyl fabric (red)

GLITTER:

* Hexagonal (red)

Template page 198

Glitter 101+

Make a matching red bow for Toto, Dorothy's dog by enlarging the bow template, following the same method as the bow on the shoe and pinning it to the dogs collar or dog coat.

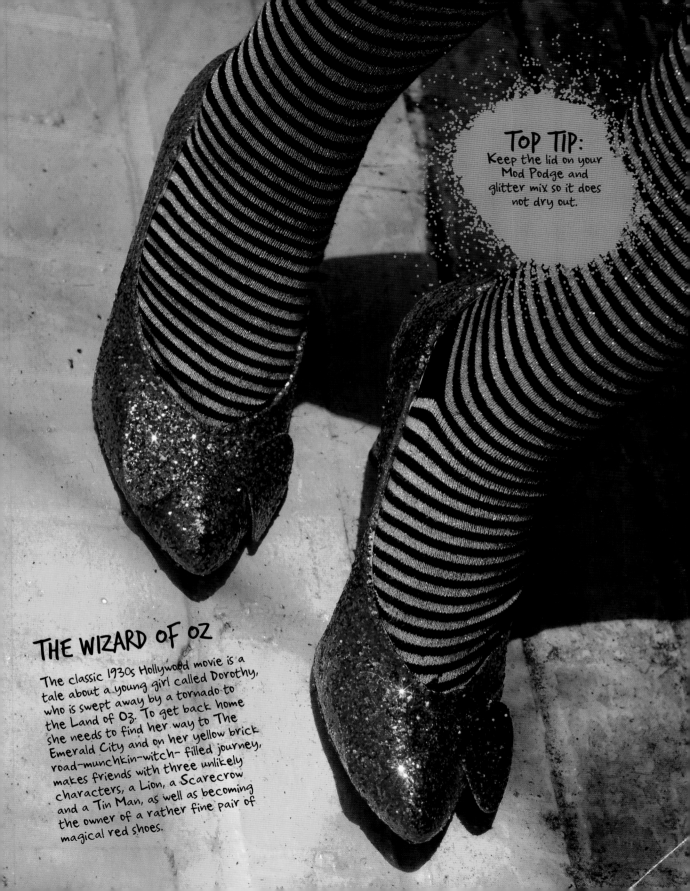

TOP TIP:

Keep the lid on your Mod Podge and glitter mix so it does not dry out.

THE WIZARD OF OZ

The classic 1930s Hollywood movie is a tale about a young girl called Dorothy, who is swept away by a tornado to the Land of Oz. To get back home she needs to find her way to The Emerald City and on her yellow brick road-munchkin-witch- filled journey, makes friends with three unlikely characters, a Lion, a Scarecrow and a Tin Man, as well as becoming the owner of a rather fine pair of magical red shoes.

DIAMONDS ARE FOREVER

Create a sparkling crystal studded winter wonderland in your hair with frosted hair claws fit for a snow queen.

CRAFT STASH:

* Plastic hair claw
* PVA glue
* Small paintbrush
* Tweezers
* Toothpick
* Swarovski crystals or acrylic gemstones
* Soft cloth

GLITTER:

* Tinsel

MAKE IT:

1 Cover one outer side of the claw with a medium layer of PVA glue. Sprinkle on tinsel glitter and shake off the excess.

2 Keep an eye on the glue, it may slide down the claw forming clumps, to prevent this, brush the glue back up and re-apply glue and glitter to any gaps that may have formed. As it starts to dry you can stand the claw up on its teeth and leave it to dry fully.

3 Repeat the process on the other outer half.

4 Again fill any gaps with additional glitter. It can look effective to have some areas covered more heavily than others so don't worry if it looks uneven.

5 When the claw is dry, apply random dots of PVA glue with a toothpick to one side. Lift each crystal up with your tweezers, position on the glue dot and press down on it to hold in place. When dry, you can do the same on the other side.

6 You're now ready to pin up your hair for a glistening night on the town.

TOP TIP:
You will find that glitter lands on the teeth and inside the claw, wipe these loose strands away for a cleaner finish.

Glitter 101+
Sparkle up a wig with a quick spritz of glitter hairspray.

FANCY FOOTWORK

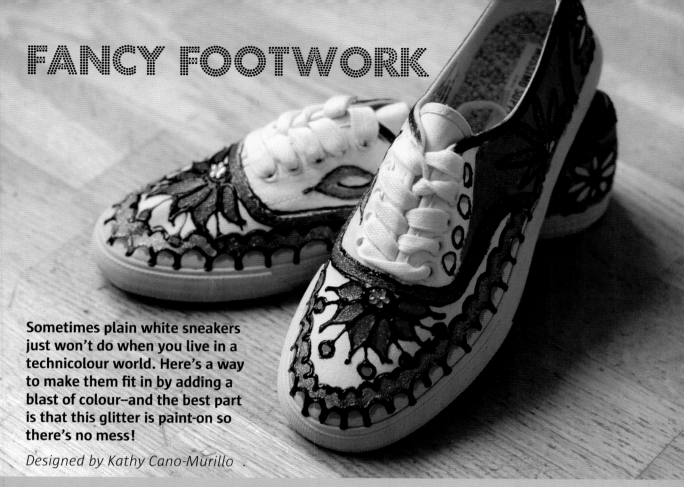

Sometimes plain white sneakers just won't do when you live in a technicolour world. Here's a way to make them fit in by adding a blast of colour--and the best part is that this glitter is paint-on so there's no mess!

Designed by Kathy Cano-Murillo

CRAFT STASH:

* 1 pair of canvas sneakers
* 3D fabric paint tube (black)
* Assorted fabric markers
* Flat back crystals
* Strong glue
* Pencil

GLITTER:

* Fabric glitter paint

MAKE IT:

1. Lightly draw your design on the shoes using a pencil.

2. Trace over your lines with the fabric paint tubes and allow to dry.

3. Fill in the areas all over the shoes with the fabric markers.

4. Apply glitter paint on top.

5. Glue on flat back crystals for extra sparkle.

Glitter 101+

Use glitter fabric paint to shimmer up wintery items like scarves, woolly hats and gloves so that you can be snug and sparkling at the same time.

TOP TIP:

If you are not confident drawing straight onto the shoe, cut out shapes or templates and draw around them.

35

HORNY DEVIL

Halloween is a good excuse to host a party. If you're too busy to think about what to wear because your time is being used to fill the bath tub with bobbing apples and hanging pom-pom spiders, then try this quick, costume idea for he-devils and she-devils: wear red from neck to toe and sew yourself this spooky headwear to complete the look.

Designed by Hatastic!

CRAFT STASH:
* Satin headband (black, 10mm/.4in)
* Paper
* Pencil
* Sharp scissors
* Cotton thread (red)
* Small bag of wadding
* Fabric glue
* Sewing machine

GLITTER:
* Glitter fabric (Josy Rose)

Template page 205

MAKE IT:

1. Copy the template onto paper and cut it out.

2. Pin the template onto the back of the glitter fabric and draw round it.

3. Repeat this on the same side, then turn the template over and draw round the template on the opposite side. Do this twice.

4. Using sharp scissors, cut out the four horn halves making sure you cut along the line you have drawn.

5. Put the two halves together so the glitter is on the outside, and overstitch the edges on a sewing machine whilst leaving 10mm/.4in at the base of the horn unsewn. Do the same with the other two halves. Leave the cotton thread that is left over from sewing the sides, as you will need this later.

6. Take a small amount of wadding and pack it into the tip of the horn and gradually pack more and more wadding in so the horn feels firm and rigid. Do the same with the other horn.

7. Then with the root of the horn that was left unsewn, fold the flaps in on themselves to seal the base. Keep the cotton thread at the sides free whilst you do this. Dab a bit of fabric glue under the first flap to stick to the wadding and then once dry, glue the other flap on top of the first flap. Hold until dry.

8. Place the horns on the hairband at the width you want them (making sure the horns face inwards) and sew the edges of the horns onto the hairband with the cotton thread you left uncut. Once they are secure, sew along the base of the horns so both are completely rigid and and get ready to scare!

TOP TIP:
Make a similar headband with different cut outs, such as two snowballs for winter. You'll need to cut out four circular pieces of silver glitter fabric or white fabric and make as above.

GLITTER 101+ Halloween ideas

* Coat toffee apples in a layer of edible glitter

* Use black glitter to make bat and cat motifs sparkle

* Transform your face with glittery face paints

* Spray trick or treat baskets with glitter spray

* Sparkle up a carved pumpkin with glitter glue spots

* Tie and hang glitter yarn to make attractive looking spider webs

* Blend up some fake blood using corn syrup, red food colouring and a touch of red edible glitter

THIS CHARMING HAND

For jewellery makers, entering a bead store is heaven. Row upon row of jars filled with plastic wonders, boxes brimming full of unusual wooden shapes, cut crystals dangling from hooks and shimmering stones in every shade of the rainbow are on display. Yet as desirable and impressive as they are, did you know that making beads is as easy as shopping for them? Not convinced? Then try this project!

Designed by Raye McKown

CRAFT STASH:

* Air-dry clay
* Cookie/clay cutters
* Craft hole punch, plastic straw or pencil
* Acrylic paints
* Rub-on transfers
* Gloss glaze/varnish
* Sparkly gems and flower embellishments
* Ribbon or jewellery findings and chain
* Buttons
* Paintbrush
* Glue
* Rolling pin
* Greaseproof paper/ baking parchment

GLITTER:

* Ultrafine

MAKE IT:

1. Roll out a piece of clay to a thickness of about 4cm/1.5in.

2. Cut out shapes with the cookie cutters.

3. Make two holes at the ends of each one using either a craft hole punch, plastic straw or end of a pencil.

4. Paint one side of the clay with acrylic paint and leave to dry, turnover and repeat.

5. Rub-on transfer wording or an image.

6. Paint glaze on one side of the clay, sprinkle with glitter and leave to dry then repeat on the reverse.

7. Glue on embellishments.

8. Thread ribbon through the beads and tie with a bow to make a bracelet or attach jump rings, a chain and metal fastenings.

TOP TIP:
Omit the holes, and glue onto a ring base.

GOT A BEADY EYE?

Turn to page 152 to see how to make paper beads.

Glitter 101+

Paint your shoelaces with a layer of glittery paint. Customise one side at a time then iron to fix.

MASTER IT!

See page 25 for more information about how to use air-dry clay.

STARLIGHT EXPRESS

Take centre stage wearing a sparkly pendant made from resin.

Designed by Gemma Andrews

CRAFT STASH:

* Gedeo Crystal Resin (or other two-part clear epoxy resin)
* Iridescent star shapes (pale blue)
* Pendant findings (e.g., a peg and loop with bail or stick-on bail)
* Resin pendant mould
* Measuring cups
* Disposable mixing cups
* Disposable mixing sticks (lollipop sticks work well for this)
* Wet/dry sandpaper
* Lacquer spray (optional)
* Clear glue suitable for metals and plastics (optional)

GLITTER:

* Fine (royal blue, black and iridescent)

MAKE IT:

1. Mix up enough resin in a cup to fill a third of your chosen mould following the manufacturer's instructions.

2. Pour the resin into your mould. Add a pinch of iridescent glitter and some stars. Use your mixing stick to carefully mix the glitter into the resin. Leave this layer to set for at least four hours.

3. Mix up another third of resin as before in a fresh cup. Pour into your mould and add a pinch of royal blue glitter and mix it into the new resin layer.

4. After letting the middle layer set for at least four hours, mix up the final layer of resin. Pour into your mould and add a light sprinkling of black glitter, carefully mixing it in.

5. Allow the resin to set completely. The time this takes can vary considerably depending on the resin manufacturer and temperature of the room. A rough guide is 24 to 48 hours.

6. When the resin has set, pop it out of the mould and use sandpaper to smooth the bottom of the pendant (the last layer you poured).

7. If required, spray the pendant with lacquer to give it extra shine.

8. Fix a bail to your pendant. If you are using a peg and loop with bail (as shown) you will need to drill a small hole in the top of your pendant before gluing it in. A stick-on bail can simply be glued onto the back. Use a glue suitable for metals and plastics.

9. Let the glue set completely then hang on your chosen chain, cord or wire to wear.

TOP TIP:

You will only need tiny amounts of resin for this project. Rather than dispose of left over resin, add more glitter to it and pour into other moulds.

CAN'T RESIST RESIN?

Turn to page 138 to see how to make a resin paperweight and see page 87 for ideas on making resin magnets

MASTER IT!

See page 28 for more information about how to use resin.

Glitter 101+

Other jewellery ideas to use with resin:

* Create glittery beads by pouring resin into small moulds and drilling a tiny hole in them so they can be threaded

* Buy a bracelet mould and use resin to create chunky plastic bangles

BAG LADY

TOP TIP: The handles are adjustable just like a bra strap so when you're stitching them inside the cups, ensure that you're not preventing any movement.

CRAFT STASH:

* Under-wired bra
* Glue gun
* Broken jewellery
* Fabric scraps
* Velcro
* Needle and thread

GLITTER:

* Glitter glue

Outgrown your bra and wondering what to do with it? Accessorise with it of course. No not literally... use simple customising techniques to transform it into an object that is beautiful and practical. Then fill it up with cash and carry it to your favourite underwear boutique to buy a new one. Don't forget to get measured properly first!

MAKE IT:

1. Cut off the bra straps and the back section of the bra where the fastening is.

2. Hold the bra closed in half so that the wire edges line up. Position one strap inside the front cup to create a handle and pin in place. Pin the second strap on the back cup creating two bag handles. With a needle and thread, stitch these in place then remove the pins.

3. Decorate the front of your bag by gluing or stitching on broken jewellery, fabric scraps and other collage materials.

4. Glue the wire edges together using a glue gun.

5. Stick or stitch a small square of Velcro inside each cup to create a closure.

6. Glitz up the final design with detailing using glitter glues.

Glitter 101+

Add a seductive shimmer to all your undies by applying dabs of fabric glue and a sprinkling of an ultrafine glitter like Glamour Dust. Iron to fix it.

GO WITH THE FLOW

A school friend of mine owned a pair of plastic jelly sandals that contained water, glitter and floating plastic Eiffel Towers inside the heel. They were the ultimate teenage fantasy. Mesmerising and magical, these water and glitter filled bangles are the closest I've ever got to those shoes. And the great thing about them is that you can wear them everyday. The heels on the other hand were so expensive she never took them out of their box.

TOP TIPS:

Opt for tubing that is soft and bendable so they are a comfy fit.

Create a matching necklace by using a larger piece of tubing. You can hide the hose lock with a ribbon if you don't want it to be seen.

MAKE IT:

1 Cut the tubing into 21cm/8in lengths (or adjust to your wrist if you want them smaller or bigger.)

2 Push one end of the hose lock into the tube. Spoon your chosen glitter inside and shake it through so you get good coverage inside the bangle. You only need a little as too much will cause blockages.

3 Fill two thirds of the tube with water, then close the tubing with the other end of the hose lock.

4 Shake up your bangle and watch as the water and glitter flow through.

CRAFT STASH:

* 3mm/ .1in diameter Plastic tubing (airline tubing for aquariums from pet shop)
* 4mm/ .15in Hose lock (garden centres)
* Spoon
* Water (mineral/distilled)
* Scissors

GLITTER:

* Of your choice

Glitter 101+

Fill your water balloons with glitter mixed with the water to add a little sparkle to your water fights.

GENTLEMAN'S CLUB

You may have to wear a plain, boring shirt to work but you can still let your personality shine through; which is the main reason cufflinks were invented. Pair up humorous words and images to make personalised cufflinks that will put a smile on your face all through the day. It's also a good way of remembering things, like important numbers, codes or clues.

CRAFT STASH:
* Cufflink findings
* Lazertran Waterslide Decal Paper (for inkjet printers)
* Image/text of your choice
* Bowl of cold water
* Greaseproof paper/ baking parchment
* Oven and tray
* Computer
* Ink jet printer
* Glue gun

GLITTER:
* Fimo or other oven hardening clay

MAKE IT:

1. Break off one small strip of Fimo and roll it in your hands until the warmth makes it manageable.

2. Roll it into a ball. Split the ball in two, each half will become one of your cufflinks.

3. Take one half, press the centre with your thumb and then use your fingers to shape and smooth the edges so you end up with small squares that measure about 1.5cm/2/3in. Place in the oven according to the instructions, on a greaseproof papered tray.

4. Decide on an image. It needs to measure at most 1.5cm/ .6in so that it fits on the Fimo square.

5. Create a digital file of the image on your computer so it can be printed off, if it is a word, the letters need to be reversed.

6. Place a sheet of Lazertran in your printer and print off the image/ text. Cut it out how you want it to be seen (any white edges you leave will show up.)

7. Put it in a bowl of cold water until the image slides off the paper (a few seconds).

8. Separate the image from the backing paper then smooth directly onto the Fimo square, position it exactly where you want it to be. You can only reposition while it is wet so make sure you are happy.

9. When dry, coat with a layer of varnish to seal, then glue the fimo tiles onto your cufflink findings.

Use glittery Fimo to add pizzazz to your cutlery. Turn to page 129 to see how

MASTER IT!

See page 25 for more information about how to use Fimo.

Glitter 101+

Add a cheeky glittery finish to your briefcase by painting it with a coat of glitter varnish and take it along to important meetings.

TOP TIP:

If you do not have a printer, take your image and Lazertran to a copy shop where they can print it for you.

CHIC CHAPEAU

With its vintage veiling and silver embellishments, this bridal fascinator is so irresistible you'll never want to take it off! Flamboyant feathers add an elegant touch making you feel like a total glamour puss.

Designed by Hatastic!

CRAFT STASH:

* Silver hat base (comb included, 9cm/3.5in)
* .5m/20in Diamante trim (4mm/.2in width)
* Feather biots (2) (small bunches of feathers used in millinery)
* Buttons (3)
* Wired diamante (1 pack)
* Grey satin ribbon (1m/1yd, 5mm/1/4in)
* Needle and cotton

GLITTER:

* Silver veiling (1m/36in)

MAKE IT:

1 Take your diamante trim and knot one end with the grey ribbon and then wrap the grey satin ribbon around each stone on the trim. You will probably need to wrap around approx 30cm/12in, measuring it against the edge of the hat base. Cut and knot at the other end.

2 Sew this trim onto the edge of the hat base, starting at the back, measuring it against the comb underneath. (The area behind the comb where the teeth face away.)

3 Take your veiling and cut 60cm/24in off the length, gather it up on one side and sew on the top of the hat base at the back, where the trim ends meet.

4 Take your two feather biots and tie them end-to-end with the wired diamante. Sew this in place at the back of the hat base again.

5 Add your three buttons in any way that you feel looks pretty!

Glitter 101+

Cover a thin plastic hair band in PVA glue then sprinkle on glitter in your favourite shade to liven up any hair do in an instant.

HERE COMES THE BRIDE

Weddings should be as personalised as possible especially when it comes to your outfit. Stamp on your character with some decorative doodling to add a flamboyant touch to your wedding accessories like these silky satin gloves, that have been given a mehndi makeover.

MAKE IT:

1 Iron the gloves so they are free of creases and lie flat.

CRAFT STASH:
* Satin wedding gloves
* Fine tip applicator
* PVA glue
* Card
* Dry brush
* Iron
* Hot Fix Swarovski Crystals and applicator

GLITTER:
* Ultrafine (Deco Art Glamour Dust in Crystal)

2 Cut a strip of card that fits snugly inside the glove leading from the hand to the edge, do not worry about the fingers. If you have purchased a new pair of gloves they will come with card already inside them, if this is the case, reinsert that card after the ironing.

3 Using the fine tip applicator, filled with PVA glue, get doodling! Customise the gloves in any pattern you want – do this freehand, whatever comes to mind. You may want to create a branching shape that starts from the edge and grows up to the fingertips, write words or draw motifs.

4 Only do a section at a time as the glue dries quickly. Before it does, pour on the glitter and shake off. Leave the gloves to dry for 48 hours then, using a dry brush, shake off any excess glitter that may have collected.

5 When the design is complete, the gloves are ready to wear. For added opulence, apply gemstones like these Hot Fix Swarovski Crystals that have been applied using a Hot Fix Applicator.

Glitter 101+

Glamour Dust dries to fabrics permanently when used over a liquid glue or fabric paint. Add it to liven up other wedding accessories like your garter and even your underwear!

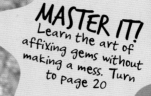
MASTER IT!
Learn the art of affixing gems without making a mess. Turn to page 20

Design inspiration:

The pattern on these gloves is based on traditional mehndi designs which are applied to the hands of the bride at South Asian Weddings; a popular beauty ritual in India, Bangladesh and Pakistan. A natural dye, it is made from crushed henna leaves that are made into a paste and applied from a cone a bit like the fine tip applicator. A modern twist on this concept, here the mehndi patterns appear on the gloves rather than the bride's hands. Most brides have bespoke patterns created to compliment their outfit and modern brides don't just restrict mehndi to their hands, it's also seen on feet, arms and even their midriff.

SHE WAS A SHOWGIRL...

For the ultimate in theatrical performance, twirl these delicate nipple tassels to bring the spirit of burlesque to your dance floor routines.

Designed by Talulah Blue

CRAFT STASH:

* Fabric glue
* Faux leather
* Tassels
* Hairgrips (10)
* Scissors
* Needle and thread
* Double-sided body tape (available from lingerie stores)

GLITTER:

* Glitter card (black)

Template page 204

MAKE IT:

1. Copy the heart template onto the back of the faux leather and cut out two pieces.

2. Glue the tab to the heart to create a cone shape. Make sure the faux leather is inside cone, as this is the bit you will apply to your body.

3. Slide the hairgrips onto your cones to hold the tab in place and leave to dry for a few hours then remove them.

4. Take a piece of glitter card that is bigger than your heart. Make a straight cut into the centre, then create another cone shape, add glue to the over lapping card and as before, use hairgrips to hold it in place until the glue dries.

5. Once the glitter top and faux leather are dry, dot glue all over the top of your heart and place your glitter cone on top, lining up the seams, the point of your heart cone and your glitter cone. Again use hairgrips to hold them together, leave to dry then remove them.

6. Use your heart base as a guide to trim the glitter card into the heart shape.

7. Sew your tassel onto the centre of the heart.

8. To wear, attach double-sided body tape to the faux leather side, press the nipple tassels onto your body and get twirling!

TOP TIP:
This heart is an average size, enlarge or decrease to suite your body.

Glitter 101+

As well as tassels, every burlesque performer needs a feather fan as part of her routine. Sparkle yours up by adding glitter along the veins and get shimmying.

THIS HOLLYWOOD LIFE

Stroll down the high street as through you are wandering the most famous boulevard in America. You may not find your name cast in the paving slabs but you will feel like a superstar.

Did you know?

Hollywood is also referred to as a Tinseltown – clearly a place full of sparkliness!

CRAFT STASH:

* Pair of flip-flop sandals
* PVA glue
* Glue gun
* Masking tape
* Paintbrush

GLITTER:

* Ultra fine (black and red)
* Foam (gold)
* Glitter glue tube (multi)

Template page 199

MAKE IT:

1 Start by decorating the thong of your flip-flop. Cover the edges where they meet the foam sandal with masking tape. Then paint on a layer of PVA glue, sprinkle the first glitter colour all over, shake it off and leave it to dry. Remove the tape.

2 Paint the edges of the sandal with PVA and sprinkle the second glitter colour all the way around. If any gaps show up after they are dry then add a second coat.

3 To create the centrepiece, use the template to cut a star from glitter foam. Affix to the thong with a glue gun and finish by writing the words 'film' and 'star' in the middle using the glitter glue.

TOP TIP:

If you can't find glitter foam, make it yourself. Turn to page 23 to find out how.

Glitter 101+

Transform the plain wedge of a high-heeled sandal by covering it in PVA glue, sprinkling on your favourite glitter, several layers for full coverage, then spraying on an adhesive to fix the glitter.

TAKE A BOW

There is nothing nerdy about wearing a bow tie, though when you do, it automatically smartens up your appearance and makes you look intelligent. That's a good enough excuse to make and wear one.

CRAFT STASH:

* Spotty cotton fabric
* Iron on interfacing
* Iron
* Needle and thread
* Dress making pins
* Sewing machine (optional)
* Thin elastic

GLITTER:

* Glitter glues

TOP TIP:
Pressing with an iron at each stage creates a crisper finish and helps your bow tie take shape more easily so don't leave these stages out!

MAKE IT:

1. Cut out the pieces of fabric that you will need. One rectangle that measures 38x7.5cm/ 15x3in, two rectangles that are 25.4x7.5cm/10x3in and a fourth piece that measures 6.3x10cm/ 2.5x4in. In addition cut one piece of interfacing that measures 25.4x7.5cm/10x3in.

2. Iron the interfacing on the reverse of one of the 25.4cm/10in by 7.5cm/3in rectangles to stiffen it.

3. Apply glitter glue to the dots, choosing colours that match and allow to dry.

4. Place the two equal sized rectangles right sides together. Sew around the edges leaving a 6mm/0.25in seam allowance and one of the short ends open. If it helps, you can pin these two pieces together first, so they do not move while you are sewing.

5. Turn the fabric inside out through the gap, and push out all the corners.

6. Press it with an iron to flatten it, then top-stitch the open end closed; making sure the edges are folded in.

7. Fold the two ends to the centre and press them closed. Then fold the whole piece in half horizontally so there is a fold going through the centre of the piece and again, press with the iron to define the fold.

8. Sew a 2.54cm/1in line, 1cm/0.5in from the bottom through the middle of the bow, it will cut through the centre fold.

9. Fold the remaining smaller rectangle in half lengthwise, put the right sides together and stitch 6mm/0.25in in, just along the length, then turn it through and press.

10. Wrap the strip over the centre of the bow so the raw ends meet at the back. Pinch them together then sew across the edge. Your bow tie will have now taken shape.

11. To complete, measure around your neck to work our how long you want the elastic to be, cut a length of elastic, feed it through the loop at the back of the bow created by the centre section, and tie into a knot. Move the knot around so it's hidden behind the centre.

GLITTER 101+

It's not just bow ties that should sparkle, glitz up an ordinary tie by adding glitter glues to emphasize the motifs.

When to wear your bow tie:

* If you are putting on a magic show

* At a picnic

* Visiting someone who needs cheering up (especially if they are in hospital)

* Going somewhere smart

* To a dinner party

CRAFT STASH:
* A t-shirt or other garment of your choice which has an image on it
* Newspaper/newsprint or other scrap paper or card
* Iron

Caring for your garment

Like any garment that has a handmade touch, it is best to wash it by hand rather than put it through the vigorous spins of a washing machine. Soak in warm soapy water then rinse.

7 SIMPLE WAYS TO MAKE YOUR GARMENTS GLITTER

MAKE IT:

Start by ironing your garment before you work on it to ensure there are no creases that can create an uneven effect. Then place the paper or card inside the garment so the glue doesn't seep through to the reverse. Images are perfect for embellishing with glitter as you can bring out the details just like this t-shirt depicting Brighton Pier. Whether you've got a pattern, text or a photograph on your garment, go to town as much or as little as you want to make it something you'll want to wear and show off with pride.

How to glitter a garment

Glitter glue: Hi-density glitter glues like Glitz It Sparkles, Tulip and Hi-Tak can be applied to a design and when dry, fixed on the back using a hot iron.

Fabric glue and fine glitter: Fabric glue looks like PVA but has a tackier consistency, you can spread it straight onto your garment and then pour on a fine glitter like Deco Art Glamour Dust. It will set permanently. Crafty Chica Extreme Embellishment Glue works wonders.

Glitter fabric marker pens: There are numerous fabric marker pens on the market with which you can draw designs and write words straight onto garments just as you would with a felt tip pen on paper. Look out for glittery pens like UHU Textile Colours and Carioca Sparkle Glitter 3D fabric paint.

Glitter fabric paint: Comes in tubes and jars and can be painted onto your clothes like normal fabric paint and then set with an iron. Try Colour Splash.

Iron-on transfer: Iron-on glitter comes in sheets or motifs that can be ironed directly onto your clothing. The sheets can be cut to size depending on the

design you would like to create. Tulip Fashion Glitter Shimmer Transfer Sheets are just right for the job.

Fabric spray paint: Glitter spray paint is perfect for use with stencils, just remember to mask off any areas you do not want to get glittery. Try Tulip Glistening Diamond Glitter Fabric Spray.

Decoupage medium specifically for fabric: Paint a coat over your glittery design to seal it in. Try Mod Podge for fabric.

DANCING QUEEN

Wiggle your hips Bollywood style with this shimmering, shiny sequin studded belt, guaranteed to turn any dance diva into an A List item number girl.

CRAFT STASH:

* Belt
* PVA glue
* Glue gun
* Masking tape
* Paintbrush
* Sequins
* Spray adhesive

GLITTER:

* Fluorescent (orange)

TOP TIP:

Take your time when it comes to gluing around the strap as you don't want to close it. Make sure there is a gap between the strap and belt while it is drying.

MAKE IT:

1. Lay the belt out flat and cover the reverse side with masking tape to prevent glitter from sticking there.

2. Turn it over and cover the front side in PVA glue. Make sure you have paper underneath the entire belt as this is a project that will get messy!

3. Apply the glitter across the entire belt. Shake off any excess and leave to dry before applying a second and possibly third coat if required.

4. Spray the front side of the belt with spray adhesive to fix the glitter and remove the masking tape.

5. Glue the sequins spaced out evenly along the belt with the glue gun so they hold.

What is an item girl?

No Bollywood film is complete without a major hit song, performed by a beautiful female star with the perfect physique and a signature shimmy. In early films, regular item girls included cabaret performer Helen, while in more recent years A List superstars have been booked to make special guest appearances.

GLITTER 101+

Transform the plain wedge of a high-heeled sandal by covering it in PVA glue, sprinkling on your favourite glitter; several layers for full coverage, then spraying on an adhesive to fix.

BIRD OF THE BALL

Make a flying entrance into party season with this dazzling peacock mask: bobbing around and showing off your feathers to attract a mate is optional.

CRAFT STASH:
* Blank mask (available from craft shops, normally made of card)
* Acrylic paint (green)
* Fine tip applicator
* PVA glue
* Dry paintbrush
* Peacock feathers (optional)

GLITTER:
* Glitter glue tubes: green and dark blue
* Holographic: turquoise
* Fine: Light green and aqua
* Standard: purple

TOP TIP:
For a Peacock Queen/ Peacock Man superhero mask, leave it as is, or transform it into a costume piece for an evening masked ball by gluing on real peacock feathers.

MASTER IT!
See page 26 for more advice about painting.

GLITTER 101+
Spray craft feathers with glitter spray and pin in your hair using grips, as a striking alternative to wearing flowers.

MAKE IT:

1. Paint your mask green.

2. Transfer the peacock eye motif randomly over the mask and outline each motif with dark blue glitter glue.

3. Line the edge of the mask with glitter glue (use dark blue for the main edge and green around the eyes).

4. Fill in each part of the eye motif, one section at a time by applying PVA glue, sprinkling glitter on top, shaking off the excess and leaving it to dry. In this sequence, purple is used at the bottom, green in the middle and turquoise for the top.

5. Use a fine tip applicator to draw on the soft feathery details that you find on the stems of peacock feathers. Pour on fine glitter, shake off and leave to dry. Remove excess glitter caught in any grooves caused by the paint with a dry paintbrush.

SHADY BUSINESS

Statement sunglasses were made for the dance floor and these are no exception. Don't worry if you can't see much through them, they are meant to bring an air of mystery to you, along with plenty of attention from admirers.

CRAFT STASH:

* Plastic sunglasses
* PVA glue
* Soft cloth and glasses cleaner
* Small acrylic gemstones
* Tweezers
* Toothpick
* Paintbrush

GLITTER:

* Superfine (royal blue)

MAKE IT:

1. Give the glasses a quick clean to make sure the surfaces are grease free.

2. Place them so the frames are facing upwards onto a sheet on paper, with the earpieces folded underneath.

3. Apply PVA glue all along the plastic frames, ensuring it is applied evenly so there are no lumpy sections.

4. Pour glitter all over, shake the excess off onto the paper and leave to dry.

5. Apply a second and third coat in the same way until you are happy with the coverage. When dry, turn the glasses around so the earpieces are facing upwards. Glitter these in the same way until the entire frame is covered in glitter.

6. Wipe the lens clean of any loose glitter then apply dots of PVA glue in lines directly on the lens. Place a gemstone in each dot using tweezers and press down with a toothpick.

TOP TIP:

If applying the gemstones makes the frames look messy, you can tidy up any gluey marks using a dampened cotton bud.

GLITTER 101+

Feeling daring? You don't just have to spangle up your sunnies - what's stopping you adding sparkle to your reading glasses or even your every day pair?

'WHY DOES IT ALWAYS RAIN ON ME?'

If you ever get the feeling that sentiment was written for you, then this is the ideal reusable shopping bag. Use it to carry a brolly around so you never get caught in a downpour again.

Designed by Louise Bird

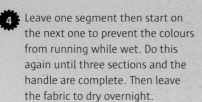

MAKE IT:

1 Enlarge the umbrella template to the size of your choice. Position it on the front side of the bag and slip a flat plastic or wooden board inside. This will give you a solid base on which to paint and prevents glue from seeping through to the other side.

2 Trace around the template with chalk, then remove the template and draw in the umbrella segments.

3 To paint each section, start with the one furthest away from the hand you are using. With the nozzle, glue a straight line to mark the boundary of that section, then squeeze a generous amount into the middle. Use a brush to spread it out evenly until the section is covered.

4 Leave one segment then start on the next one to prevent the colours from running while wet. Do this again until three sections and the handle are complete. Then leave the fabric to dry overnight.

5 Fill in the remaining segments in the same way. When the entire bag is dry, turn it over and iron on the reverse, this sets the glue and flattens the pattern.

CRAFT STASH:
* Plain cotton bag
* Fabric chalk
* Plastic or wooden board
* Paintbrush

GLITTER:
* High-density glitter glue such as Glitz It, Hi-Tack or Pebeo in blue, silver, red and gold

Template page 201

TOP TIP:
If you haven't achieved the density of glitter you want, go over the pattern a second time but only once the first layer is dry.

GLITTER 101+

Use the same technique to sparkle up soft furnishings like cushion covers and curtains.

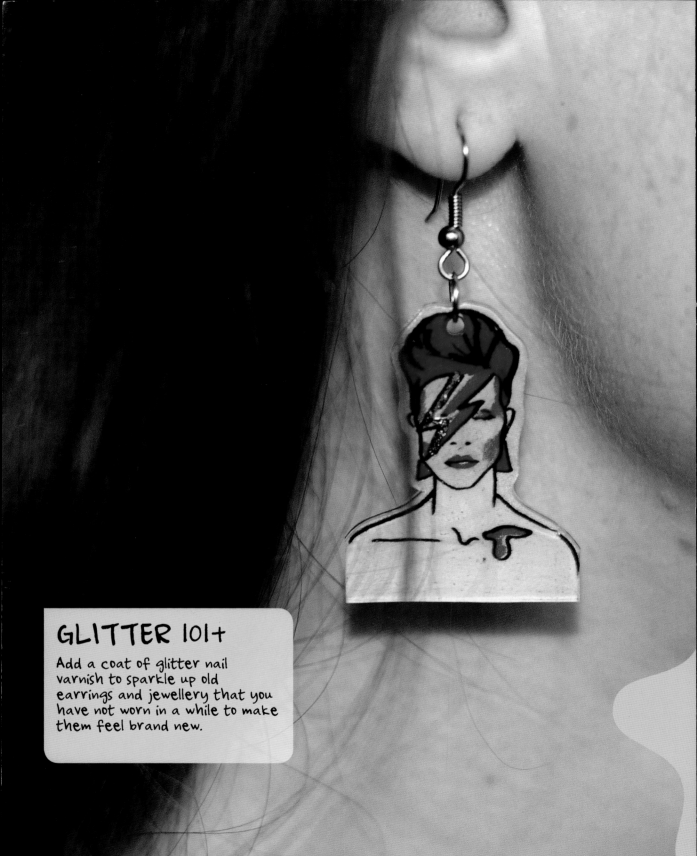

GLITTER 101+

Add a coat of glitter nail varnish to sparkle up old earrings and jewellery that you have not worn in a while to make them feel brand new.

PLASTIC FANTASTIC

Shrink plastic is a miracle product! Use it to turn your illustrations into wearable art like these too uber cool Ziggy Stardust earrings. Just draw, colour and heat.

Designed by Ruth Crean

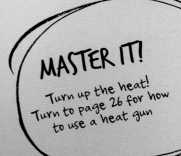

MASTER IT!
Turn up the heat! Turn to page 26 for how to use a heat gun

CRAFT STASH:
* 1 Sheet of Shrinkles Shrink Plastic (A6 size, frosted)
* Marker pen (Sharpie, black)
* Scissors
* Paper punch
* Colouring pencils
* Heat gun or oven
* Earwires x 2
* Silver jump rings x 2
* Jewellery making pliers x2

GLITTER:
* Nail varnish

TOP TIP:
If you are not confident at drawing, try to scale down images you see online, there is lots of great clip art that would make fun jewellery. Or draw abstract circles and shapes and have fun with different colour combinations.

MAKE IT:

1. Start by drawing a template of the design you want to turn into earrings; it does not need to be a 1970s pop star.

2. Cut your sheet of Shrink Plastic in half horizontally.

3. Place one of the halves over your template with the rough side facing up. Using the marker, trace around the image. Any words will need to be reversed, so if you are including any text; write it backwards.

4. Use colouring pencils to shade the image. For white areas, a white pencil must be used.

5. Repeat steps 2-5 again with the other half of the shrink plastic, trying to keep the two images matching so you have two identical earrings.

6. Cut around both of your shapes leaving a 3mm/.1in border.

7. Using your paper punch, punch a hole about 5mm/.2in in from the top. This takes practise as if you go too far in, your jump ring will not fit, and if you come too far out, you are in danger of ruining the connection; so test on a sample first. Always punch your hole before heating; it cannot be done afterwards.

8. You can your shrink plastic in two ways:

   Oven: Preheat your oven to 170°C/340°F, cover a baking tray with tinfoil and place your drawings rough side down. Place in the oven and watch through the glass as your drawing shrinks in size. At this point your item may curl up, give it an extra minute and wait for it to flatten out. Remove from the oven and quickly use a flat surface like the bottom of a glass to press down and flatten the pieces. They will be hot to the touch.

   Heat gun: Shrink one at a time. Place your drawing in a baking tray and direct your heat gun at it. The drawing will move around, follow the movement with your gun. When it has stopped shrinking, use a flat block to flatten your drawing.

9. When they have cooled, paint on a layer of glitter nail varnish to add detail to the design.

10. To assemble the earring use two pliers. Open up a jump ring and place it through the hole in the top of the drawing then attach your silver earwire. With your pliers, close the ring back together. Repeat the step for the other earring.

ACCEPTABLE IN THE 80S

Power dressing doesn't just mean wearing slick suits: it's about making a statement. One way to get noticed is by modelling a larger than life pair of shoulder pads – these ones will transform you into a centre stage pop diva.

CRAFT STASH:
* 2 m/ 6.5ft of wide ribbon
* Threads to match tulle
* Scissors
* Elastic band x 2
* Sewing machine

GLITTER:
* Tulle net fabric
* 2 x pieces for inner colour 31cm/12in width by 165.5cm/65in length
* 2 x pieces for outer colour 62cm/24in width by 165.5cm/65in length

MAKE IT:

1. Take your inner piece of tulle, fold it in half lengthways and then loosely pleat it into a concertina.

2. Remove the foot from your sewing machine so it doesn't get caught in the net. Using a wide, loose running stitch, sew over the rough (not the folded) edge of the concertina. As you approach the end of the concertina, fold up the rest of the net in concertina fashion as you feed it through the sewing machine so that the whole length is stitched across.

3. Repeat this with one of your outer pieces so you end up with two ruffled pieces of tulle, both the same length with the outer piece double the width of the inner piece.

4. Line up the edges of both pieces and then join them together by sewing a loose running stitch creating a two-layered ruffle. Sew up the ends so they both meet, creating a circular ruffle.

5. Form a 'bouquet' shape by pulling the inner part of the ruffle downward – you will notice that it starts to look like a giant flower or corsage. Secure the end of the 'bouquet' with an elastic band (underneath the flower shape). Repeat with your other two pieces of tulle so that you end up with two identical corsage shapes. These will become your shoulder pads.

6. Hold the ribbon across your back and mark off the centre point (your neck) then make a mark for where each of your shoulders are and tie the pads in place.

7. To wear the shoulder pads, position the pads on your shoulder, take the ribbon around to the back and tie them up to form a bow (you made need someone to help you do this!)

GLITTER 101+
Tie strips of glitter tulle net along a piece of ribbon and tie it around your waist creating a sparkling grass skirt.

If you're worried you'll end up looking like actresses Joan Collins and Linda Evans from the 1980s soap opera Dynasty, then don't worry. Shoulder pads actually came into fashion in the post-war 1940s era which means they are actually vintage and not bad taste!

BE THE EYE OF THE TIGER...

...and show them who's boss down at the gym. Though don't be surprised if you start getting orders from your fitness buddies. Luckily with super simple iron-on glitter you won't need to duck away. You will be pulling out the punches on these delightful vests in no time.

TOP TIP: Handwash this top as normal in warm soapy water, do not wring it too much or put it in a washing machine.

MAKE IT:

1 Start with the boxing glove template, draw around it on the reverse side of the iron-on glitter sheet, cut it out and put it to the side. (The top side has a plastic coating.)

2 Next do the letters. Cut a piece of fusible webbing that is slightly larger than all the letter templates if they were laid out, but smaller than your blue felt. With the paper side facing towards you and glue side down, iron the webbing onto the felt. When cool, place the letter templates on the paper side, draw around them, cut them out then peel off the paper so you are left with letters with a shiny glue base. Again put aside.

3 Repeat this same technique with the red motif.

4 Position the glove on your vest, place a tea towel on top and iron over it quickly and smoothly applying even pressure. It will only take a few seconds to bond so keep an eye on it to make sure it does not burn. Leave it to cool down completely before you peel off the plastic coating revealing the glittery glove.

5 Position the red motif glue side down and iron over the entire design paying particular attention to all the pointy corners. Again it won't take long to affix to the vest. If you are worried about burning or staining the fabric, place a thin piece of cloth over the satin before you iron.

6 Do the same with the blue felt letters, ironing them on one at a time.

7 Turn the vest inside out and iron over the reverse of the design.

8 When the vest has completely cooled, line the edges of the satin motif with a tube of gold glitter glue to ensure the edges are defined, and the design does not fray.

CRAFT STASH:

* Plain vest/t-shirt (ironed to remove creases)
* Sharp scissors
* Satin fabric (red)
* Felt (blue)
* Iron
* Paper backed iron on fusible webbing (HeathnBond Ultra Hold)
* Pencil
* Ruler
* Card
* Tea towel
* Thin fabric scrap (optional)

GLITTER:

* Sheet of iron-on glitter (Hot Fix from Ki-Sign)
* Glitter glue (Gold)

Template page 195

GLITTER 101+

Use a glitter glue tube to write your name inside your clothes so they can't go missing!

CUT & PASTE CLUTCH

Introducing the easiest appliqué ever...

CRAFT STASH:
* Clutch bag (or other textile, garment or bag)
* Cotton fabric with motifs
* Fabric glue
* Sharp scissors

GLITTER:
* Hi-density glitter glue

MAKE IT:

1 Cut shapes, motifs, words or designs from your cotton fabric. For this design, love hearts were cut out individually.

2 Scatter these over the clutch bag or your chosen item and stick them in place using fabric glue ensuring all the edges are smoothed down.

3 To seal the motifs, edge them with a line of glitter glue.

GLITTER 101+
Try this method on:
* Towels
* Hankies
* Socks
* Bibs
* Gloves
* Woolly hats
* Pockets
* Pants
* Pillowcases and anything else you want to customise quickly

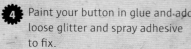

ALL BUTTONED UP

So many buttons, so many ideas....so take your time deciding how to customise them.

MAKE IT:

1 Use glitter glue in tubes to draw shapes, patterns, stripes, spots, circles.

2 Glue on gems or sequins for added shininess

3 Cover the whole button in a coat of glue for a glittery varnished finish.

4 Paint your button in glue and add loose glitter and spray adhesive to fix.

CRAFT STASH:
* Assortment of buttons
* Glittery sequins, gemstones
* PVA glue
* Spray adhesive

GLITTER:
* Glitter glues in different colours
* Any type of loose glitter

SHAKE YOUR POMPOMS

A wonderfully fluffy necklace that is comfy to wear and will make admirers want to come up and say hello. Once you have mastered the knack of making a pom pom there are infinite ways to incorporate them into your life. This is just the beginning...

Designed by Caz Turner

MAKE IT:

Pom poms

1. Cut the leather to determine the length. This project uses 70cm/28in for the necklace (x 2 pieces) and 25cm/10in for the bracelet.

2. Next decide how big you want the pompom to be. These pompoms are 5cm/2in in diameter.

3. Trace two circles in your chosen size onto card and cut out. Fold your circles in half, create a smaller circle in the middle and cut out. Place these two donut shaped circles together.

4. Cut your threads into lengths that will be easy to manage. (It is too hard pushing a ball of wool through the middle hole.) In these pompoms there is a mix of wool, lame thread and metallic embroidery threads.

5. Push the length through the hole in the middle then push the other end of the thread through the loops, almost creating a knot. You can now keep wrapping the thread in and out, around and around, filling up the circle very quickly.

6. You will know when you are finished when you cannot pull anymore thread through the middle hole. Thread the ends under another thread to secure.

7. Cut a 20cm/8in long piece of thread from your main colour and set aside.

8. Push apart the thread on the edge of the donut with your fingernail and separate the two cardboard pieces.

9. Snip your way around the donut. As you snip, the thread will pop out straight.

10. Once you have cut all the way around, separate the two cardboard pieces slightly more and wrap the 20cm/8in piece of wool around the centre of the pompom between the cardboard. Once wrapped, tie a very tight knot.

11. Pull the cardboard off either side revealing the pompom. Take it in your fingers and 'plump' it out making it fluffy and full.

12. To neaten the pompom, snip off the longer pieces and cut any loops so that they are separate pieces of thread.

13. Set aside and repeat the process to make as many pompoms as you want.

Making up the necklace

1. To make up the item, take your first pompom and determine where the centre of it is using your finger. Push through a small crochet hook so that it pokes out the other side.

2. Attach the leather strip onto the hook and pull through the middle. Repeat this process with the other pompoms.

3. For this necklace, you can use two lengths of leather creating two layers of pompoms.

4. When complete, knot the ends of the necklace together at the back of the neck according to the length you would like.

GLITTER 101+

Use glittery yarn for crochet projects, it gives granny squares a whole new life.

More pompom ideas

* Make large pompoms and join to make a scarf

* Create a pompom belt

* Add a pompom to tie up a gift instead of a bow

* Tie a pompom to your suitcase so you can identify it on the airport carousel

* Add eyes for a pompom with character

* Hang giant pompoms for party decorations

CRAFT STASH:

* Ball of wool and embroidery threads in a colour of your choice
* Thin leather or fabric cord (used in jewellery making) (2m/2yds)
* Jewellery findings (hooks and catchers)
* Cardboard
* Pencil
* Scissors
* Pointy nose/needle nose pliers
* Small crochet hook
* Something circular to draw around

GLITTER:

* Glittery yarn

TOP TIP:

Using a crochet hook to pull through threads makes it quicker and easier to make a fuller pompom.

HOMES & INTERIORS

TREE OF LIFE

Positive thinking is the key to having a happy and fulfilling life, and surrounding yourself in affirmations will help you achieve that. Display daily inspirations to motivate you to achieve your goals. Repeat them to yourself and change them regularly.

Designed by Fatema Hossain

CRAFT STASH:

* Artists canvas 20x25cm/8x10in
* Circular paper clips
* Pencils (Derwent metallic gold and a grey sketching pencil)
* Fine tip applicator
* PVA glue
* Glue gun
* Watercolour paints
* Small brush
* Decorative edged scissors
* Paper

GLITTER:

* Standard (red)
* Tinsel (Green)
* Holographic (gold)

Template page 197

MAKE IT:

1. Transfer the main design onto the canvas and start painting it.

2. For the ground use yellows and oranges. To create a rippled effect, work in a continuous line that starts from the outside and works inwards into each space. Do the same with the sky in blue paint and then fill in the leaves and trunk.

3. When dry, use the gold pencil to widen the branches of the tree. Go over with the fine tip applicator filled with PVA and sprinkle on the holographic glitter.

4. For the leaves, start from the inside. Apply PVA glue then sprinkle on the green tinsel glitter.

5. Use the fine tip applicator to outline the leaf edges and centre, then apply more green glitter for a 3D effect.

6. For the paperclips, paint the flat surfaces with PVA and pour on red glitter to make them look like juicy apples. Shake off the excess and leave to dry then glue them onto the tree.

7. Use decorative edged scissors to cut small pieces of paper to hang from the clips. Write in your affirmations and get ready for some life changing inspiration.

MASTER IT!

Seeking paint perfection? Turn to page 29 for painting tips

MORE ABOUT AFFIRMATIONS

When you affirm something, you confirm it in a positive manner and the more you believe in these thoughts, the more likely they are to come true. Remember, the more positive they are the better!

Glitter 101+

Write affirmations on a small pocket mirror like I am gorgeous and carry it around in your purse. Look at yourself and read it whenever you're feeling a little down.

73

NO ENTRY

Sometimes you own things that have broken but can't bear to throw them away. In crafting it's always possible to find a use for them, in fact broken jewellery, random buttons and odd knick-knacks are like treasure to me. I store them away in boxes, just as I do with special things to keep them safe. Then when a project comes along that needs something extra unusual, I know where to start. Like this one...

CRAFT STASH:

* Blank wreath (either card or polystyrene)
* Assorted collage items such as broken jewellery and knick-knacks
* Scrabble letters
* Cuddly toy
* Tissue paper (pink, orange and peach)
* PVA glue
* Water
* Paintbrush
* Scissors
* Glue gun

GLITTER:

* Foil
* Confetti glue

MAKE IT:

1. Cut the tissue paper into squares and rectangles.

2. Dilute PVA glue with water to create a runny paste and paste on the tissue paper shapes. Do one colour at a time, alternating their position between each layer to create a geometric effect.

3. While it is still wet, randomly sprinkle on the glitter.

4. Cover the whole wreath in a layer of confetti glue.

5. If any of the tissue pieces overlap the edge of the wreath, fold them over the edge and glue in place.

6. Get creative! Start with the Scrabble tiles. Glue these across the top of the wreath, spelling out My Room, using the glue gun. Then position your other collage materials around the wreath and glue into place. On this wreath there are broken key rings, earrings, brooches and hair slides.

TOP TIP:

Be very careful when you apply the tissue paper squares. They have a tendency to tear or squish up, if that happens remove them unless that is the effect you want. To create a stronger geometric design like the one created here, only use clean shapes.

GLITTER 101+

Make door signs for all your rooms from glittery funky foam (neoprene). Start with a rectangle base and tape a piece of thread on the back for a hook. Cut letters from different colours of foam spelling out rooms such as kitchen, bathroom and office and stick these on the front.

MUSIC TIME

A nifty way to put a scratched CD to use. With their pre-cut hole, light-weight, and durability, they make the perfect clock face. Just decorate and add hands.

Designed by Elisa Begg

CRAFT STASH:

* Blank or unwanted CD
* Patterned paper
* Clock mechanism and hands
* Glue
* Small pair of sharp scissors

GLITTER:

* Glue tubes

MAKE IT:

1 Cover the label side of the CD with glue right up to all the edges.

2 Place the CD glue side down onto the back of your chosen patterned paper, smoothing it out so there are no bumps. Leave to dry then carefully cut off the excess paper around the edge of the CD.

3 If you wish to put glitter on the hands it is a good idea to do that now so it has time to dry. Apply glitter glue straight from the tube, spread over the hands and allow to dry.

4 Take a pair of sharp scissors and carefully cut a small hole where the centre of the CD is.

5 Decorate the clock face. Depending on the design, embellish the shapes and patterns with sparkle and add a glittery edge.

6 After you have decorated the face and the glitter has dried add the numbers. Use clear acrylic gems. Start with the number 12 and then 3, 6 and 9. You can leave it with only the four numbers or continue and add the rest, making sure you have equal spacing.

7 Once everything is dry add the mechanism and hands. Insert the spindle of the mechanism through the clock face then attach using the small nut or washer that is supplied with the mechanism. Then gently push the hands onto the spindle starting with the hour hand, then the minute and finally the second hand.

TOP TIP:
Use vinyl records for a larger version of this project, made in exactly the same way.

GLITTER 101+

Make a compilation CD of your favourite tracks with the listings insert made from glittery paper and send to a friend you have not spoken to in a long time.

ARABIAN NIGHTS

Drift away to an exotic land filled with sweltering deserts, softly plodding camels, beautiful belly dancers and yurts filled with lavishly decorated pillows that you can rest on as you sip fresh mint tea. The latter half of this fantasy can be recreated in the luxury of your own home; pour boiling water onto fresh mint leaves and sitting back against an arabesque inspired bolster. As for the camels, that may have to wait until you are actually on holiday.

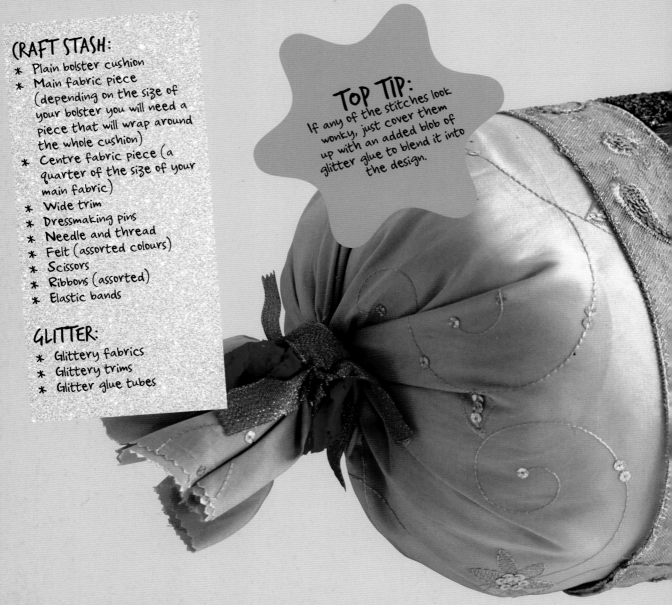

CRAFT STASH:
* Plain bolster cushion
* Main fabric piece (depending on the size of your bolster you will need a piece that will wrap around the whole cushion)
* Centre fabric piece (a quarter of the size of your main fabric)
* Wide trim
* Dressmaking pins
* Needle and thread
* Felt (assorted colours)
* Scissors
* Ribbons (assorted)
* Elastic bands

GLITTER:
* Glittery fabrics
* Glittery trims
* Glitter glue tubes

TOP TIP:
If any of the stitches look wonky, just cover them up with an added blob of glitter glue to blend it into the design.

MAKE IT:

1 Lay the bolster in the centre of your main fabric and wrap the fabric around it, overlapping the edge where they meet.

2 Use elastic bands to gather the spare fabric at each end and secure them.

3 Disguise the elastic bands by tying ribbons over them. This will also help secure the ends.

4 Turn the bolster over to where the edges of the main fabric meet. Turn over both edges to create a neat fold and pin them together.

Sew a basic running stitch by hand along this line, removing the pins as you go.

5 Pin the centre fabric across the middle, ensuring the ends meet in the same place as the main fabric, on the back and hand stitch into place as above.

6 Cut two lengths of trim that stretch across both edges of the centre section. Make sure they overlap the edge of the fabric, pin them in place and again stitch to the bolster.

7 Cut triangles from a sheet of glitter fabric and glue these opposite each other at either end of the centre section.

8 To complete the arabesque flavour, make a motif in a design of your choice using felt scraps, stitch or glue it together and highlight areas with glitter glue. Affix to the centre of the bolster.

GLITTER 101+

To make really easy no-sew fabric covers, take a cushion pad and two equal size squares of glittery fabric slightly bigger than the pad. Cut slits all along the edges of each square that are 2cm/ .8in apart so that you end up with a tassel effect all the way around. Create a sandwich by placing the pad in between both squares. Take one tassel from above and one from below and tie them together over the edge of the pad. Do this all the way along until you create a tasselled glittery cushion.

SUPERSIZE LOUNGING

Yum! It makes me feel hungry just looking at this giant burger. I grew up in the 1980s when burger-shaped beanbags were iconic. I craved one but never got it. Luckily now that I'm older I can make my own! This version is smaller, it's a footstool instead, which is stacked up using Velcro or it can be left separated to make scatter cushions. Question is: should you make fries to go with it? (They would make comfy armrests!)

MAKE IT:

1 Cut out all your fabric pieces using pinking shears to prevent fraying:

Bun – four circles of beige satin 50cm/20in diameter

Burger – two circles of fleece 48cm/18in diameter

Tomato – two circles of red 48cm/18in tinsel diameter

Cheese slice – two 42cm/16in squares of yellow satin

Lettuce – two pieces of green holographic fabric start with circles of 46cm/18in diameter but cut them with a wiggly, uneven edge to create the curly edges of a lettuce leaf.

2 For each piece hold the right sides together and pin them leaving a 5mm/.2in seam allowance. Thread your sewing machine with a matching colour and straight stitch around the edge leaving a gap so you can fill it with the beads. Remove the pins as you sew.

3 Turn the fabric inside out and make sure all the edges are pushed out. Fill up each section with beads, approx. three quarters of the way full then close the open gap with your hands and push the beads around to fill the cushion out and see if you need any more. Add as required.

4 The burger should be the most filled out section to give it a denser shape. The top of the bun also needs a lot of filling to make it look rounded, while the bottom of the bun needs less filling, giving it a flat base for the other ingredients to rest on.

5 When you have the right quantity of filling in each piece, fold in the open end and top stitch it closed.

6 Layer up the burger and if you want to use it as a stool, tape squares of Velcro between layers, or leave them separate so you can use the filling as scatter cushions.

7 For the final touch cut out some oblong 'seeds' in brown felt, top them with fabric glue and glitter, and then glue to the top of the bun.

CRAFT STASH:

* Satin fabric (beige 2m/2yds, yellow .5m/20in)
* Fleece (brown, .5m/20in)
* Sharp scissors
* Pinking sheers
* Threads in shades to match the fabrics
* Scraps of brown felt
* Fabric glue
* Velcro/ hook and loop squares (optional)
* Beanbag filling (polystyrene beads)
* Dressmaking pins
* Sewing machine (you can attempt to sew by hand, but it will take you a while)

GLITTER:

* Fabrics (red tinsel .5m/20in and green holographic .5m/20in)
* Holographic (brown)

TOP TIP:
Polystyrene beads are extremely static and will stick to your hand and start jumping around as soon as you open the bag. If possible ask someone to hold the gap in your cushion open while you pour the beads in.

GLITTER 101+

Use glittery fabric in your patchworking. It will make a change from the usual cotton squares used in quilt making resulting in a disco effect blanket.

STREET PARTY REVIVAL

The recent renaissance of afternoon tea has led to high demands for bunting; small flags that are often hung up for celebrations like street parties where tea and cake are part of the proceedings. Clay bunting offers a modern twist on this classical décor adding sophistication to all your festivities, or simply hang up, whenever you have guests over.

Designed by Raye McKown

TOP TIP: Make clay letters and spell out a name or word, perfect for decorating a child's bedroom.

GLITTER 101+

If you're creating a spread of tasty treats for an afternoon tea, make signs to help identify the menu choices with a small flag made from paper and taped onto a cocktail stick that can be placed straight into food. Use a glitter marker pen to write on what they are.

MAKE IT:

1. Roll out your clay to a thickness of about 4cm/1.5in

2. Draw a long triangle on cardboard, cut it out, place on top of the clay and cut around with a craft knife. Create as many pieces of bunting as you require.

3. Using a craft hole punch, straw or the bottom of a pencil, make two holes at each side at the top of the bunting big enough to thread a piece of ribbon through.

4. Paint one side of the clay with acrylic paint and leave to dry.

5. Turnover and repeat.

6. Paint the clay with glaze on one side and sprinkle with glitter.

7. When dry turnover and repeat.

8. Using cookie cutters, cut out shapes (hearts and butterflies) from the clay, paint with acrylic paint and allow to dry.

9. Apply glue to the tops of the shapes and sprinkle with glitter.

10. Glue sparkly gems to the butterflies and outline the edge with glue and glitter.

11. Add on other embellishments such as sequins, beads and plastic charms.

12. Thread ribbon through the holes at the top of the bunting to hang.

CRAFT STASH:

* Air-drying clay
* Cardboard
* Gloss glaze/varnish
* Variety of cookie/clay cutters
* Craft hole punch, plastic straw or pencil
* Acrylic paints
* Sequins
* Sparkly gems and flower embellishments
* Ribbon
* Paintbrush
* Glue
* Rolling pin
* Craft knife

GLITTER:

* Ultrafine

SHAKEN, NOT STIRRED... 007

If I wasn't a crafter I would be a Bond girl. A powerful femme fatale; articulate and intelligent, owning a wardrobe of slinky dresses with queues of billionaires eager to date me. But alas, I have chosen a life of glitz without the glamour, so have to make do with daydreams and themed furniture instead.

MAKE IT:

1 Measure the surface of the table and ask a professional glass cutting shop to cut you a piece of glass that size. In this example, the circular surfaces have a diameter of 42cm/16in and two were purchased, one for each layer.

2 Next paint your table. Depending on the state of it (this one was purchased in a junk shop and was in good condition), it may need some sanding down so the surface is smooth. Before you start, cover any areas you do not want to get paint on with masking tape, such as the wheels.

3 If the table comes apart separate the pieces and paint each one individually or do it in one go, using an interiors paint suitable for the material you are using. As this table was made of wood, wood paint was used, but if yours is plastic or metal, check the label.

4 You will need to apply several coats for full coverage. After the final layer of paint has dried, apply a coat of pearlescent craft glue, this is optional and is just to add some extra shine.

5 Mix together your white glitter and Mod Podge (two part glitter to one part glue) to create a grainy texture and paint the table or trolley legs to give it a crystallised look.

6 Trace your templates on the reverse of the black glitter fabric and cut them out using scissors. Next use the craft knife and mat to cut out the holes to define the body shapes. The key to using a craft knife is holding it down flat, not at a point.

7 Arrange them on the table top/s and glue into position with the glue gun. Attach the black marabou trim around the edge, also using the glue gun for additional Bond girl glamour.

8 To complete, place your bespoke cut glass piece/s on top creating the ultimate drinks table.

TOP TIP: Work outdoors when you are painting or in a well ventilated space and be patient as interior paint can take a long time to dry and you will need to apply several coats.

CRAFT STASH:

* Cocktail trolley
  or small table
* Glass sheet
* Interiors paint (white)
* Craft paint (white
  pearlescent - optional)
* Marabou trim
  (black - optional)
* Glue gun
* Paintbrushes
* White spirit
* Masking tape
* Craft knife and mat
* Scissors
* Mod Podge

GLITTER:

* Fabric (black)
* White

Templates page 207

MASTER IT!

See page 29 for more
information about how to
use paint.

GLITTER 101+

Create Bond inspired favours
for party guests by painting
small model cars (preferably
Aston Martins) with a layer of
gold glitter and PVA glue and
sealing the sparkle with a coat
of gloss or adhesive spray.

85

DUST UNDER ATTACK!

Don't let anyone ambush your spring cleaning. These soldiers have been deployed to stand guard over your sweeping, making sure your home sparkles with sheen, rather than glitter droppings.

MAKE IT:

1 Apply a strip of masking tape underneath the edges of the dustpan and paint them and the brush handle with emulsion paint, then leave to dry

2 Paint both with a layer of green acrylic paint and again leave to dry.

3 Prepare the flowers by cutting off their stems using wire cutters (most synthetic flowers have a wire base inside). Dab PVA glue randomly on each petal, front, underneath and along the edges. Add glitter, shake off the excess then allow to dry.

4 Glue the flowers to your brush handle, leaving a small gap at the end of it to allow for easier handling.

5 Paint over the green areas of the dustpan with your coloured glue then immediately sprinkle your fine green glitter all over.

6 To finish, using the glue gun affix your soldiers onto the handle and edges of your dustpan. They are ready for work; are you ready to clean?

CRAFT STASH:

* Plastic dustpan and brush
* Emulsion paint
* Acrylic paint (green)
* Coloured glue (green)
* Paintbrushes
* Synthetic flowers
* Plastic soldiers
* PVA glue
* Masking tape
* Wire cutters
* Glue gun

GLITTER:

* Extra fine (green (dustpan) and a colour to match your flowers (pink)

TOP TIP:
You can stick anything on your dustpan and brush to make doing the chores much more appealing. And don't forget to make a matching broom too!

GLITTER 101+
Create a sparkling bin by spraying the whole surface outdoors, with a can of glitter spray.

FLIGHT OF FANCY

One of Britain's best-loved interiors accessories; no suburban home was without a flock of flying ducks in the 1970s. They had mass appeal and were made from wood or ceramic. If the quirkiness of a trio of retro quacking birds doesn't appeal, try moulding something that does, to create original and kitsch fridge magnets.

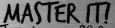

MASTER IT!
Turn to page 28 for more information about how to use resin and also to see more on making your own mould.

CRAFT STASH:
* Gedeo Siligum moulding paste
* Gedeo (or other two-part epoxy resin kit)
* Vaseline (or other petroleum jelly)
* An object to mould (small wooden duck)
* Magnet back
* Glue gun
* Sandpaper

GLITTER:
* Ultrafine

MAKE IT:

1. Moulding paste allows you to make a mould of any object. The Siligum kit consists of two gums that are blue and white. Take an equal quantity of each gum and roll them around into a ball in your hands until both colours are fully blended together.

2. Stretch and smooth this gum mix over the object you want to make a mould of. Work quickly as it sets in five minutes. You can then remove the object you were moulding and an imprint will be left behind.

3. Work out how much resin you will need to make up and ensure every corner and crease of the mould is lined with Vaseline.

4. Pour your chosen glitter into the mould, filling it two thirds and covering every part of it.

5. Mix up the resin and pour it into the mould. Some glitter may float to the top, but that is fine.

6. Leave it to dry for at least 24 hours before popping it out of the mould. If you disturb it before then, it may not have fully solidified and will lose its shape.

7. Use the sandpaper to smooth out any rough edges – in resin work, you normally find that the top layer and edges may be a bit bumpy.

8. Finally glue a magnet onto the back.

GLITTER 101+

Make fabulous fridge magnets by mixing up resin and glitter and pouring it into unusually shaped ice cube trays. When dry, pop them out, sand and glue a magnet on the back.

TOP TIP:
Each mould can be re-used up to 50 times so don't let it go to waste!

SHINE LIKE THE STARS

A candle that smells divine and looks incredible? Every home needs one! Brightly coloured bubbly gel is combined with glitter to create handmade candles that can be set inside any glass container for a fragrant, warm glow and homely ambience.

Designed by Rebecca Holder

MAKE IT:

1 Paint stars on the outside of your votive, using glass paints in yellow and white. Leave to dry (about 24 hours).

2 Take the wick and put your wick sticker underneath the metal part on the bottom, then gently place it in the glass, wick pointing up, as central as you can. Rest the chopsticks on the top of the glass to hold the wick in place.

3 You need enough gel to fill the glass, leaving about a quarter of an inch room at the top. To work out the quantity fill the glass container with water, check the amount with your measuring cup, then weigh out the gram equivalent of gel (plus a little extra).

4 Melt the wax in your metal saucepan on your hob/stove top and leave it uncovered.

5 Heat the gel to about 87°-104°C/190°-220°F. Use your thermometer to check. The hotter you heat it, the fewer bubbles, but for safety do not exceed 107°C/225°F.

6 Add fragrance. There are lots of lovely gel wax safe fragrances to choose from. Do not use a fragrance that is not gel wax safe – always check. Use it sparingly, about a tablespoon per two cups of gel. Stir it in well.

7 You can add the colour in any order you like. For this design start by stirring in some orange, only a drop so it retains some transparency.

8 Slowly pour the wax into the votive holder. Keep an eye on your wick and gently move it (from the top) if it leans to one side.

9 Sprinkle on a very small amount of your candle glitter.

10 In another pan, repeat the above process, this time with yellow dye. Pour over the cooled orange and sprinkle more glitter on top.

11 Leave the new layer to cool a little, then top up your candle with the rest of the orange gel wax, leaving a 6mm/.24in at the top.

12 Check your wick, adjust your chopsticks to keep it in place and leave it to cool.

13 Keep an eye on the wick – check it every now and again and give it a little tug in the right direction if it strays. You may need to gently pull it up, but very gently!

14 Once the wax has fully cooled, trim the visible wick. Carefully give the container a wipe with the tea towel to remove any blobs of wax on the outside. Light and enjoy!

CRAFT STASH:

* Votive holder
* Gel wax (Penreco - clear)
* Gel wax dye (yellow and orange)
* Wick (with a metal base)
* Wick stickers
* Glass paints (Vitrea 160 from Pebeo)
* Hob/stove top
* Metal saucepan (2 x small)
* Spoon
* Chopsticks
* Thermometer (a jam thermometer works well)
* Scent: Tibetan Black Tea
* Damp tea towel (just in case!)

GLITTER:

* Candle glitter (gold)

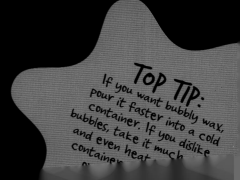

TOP TIP: If you want bubbly wax, pour it faster into a cold container. If you dislike bubbles, take it much and even heat container.

GLITTER 101+

Add glamour to dinner parties by decorating tapered candles that can rest inside empty wine bottles. Start by removing their sheen using a soft cloth dipped in white spirit. Then coat the candle in PVA and cover with candle glitter.

SILVER LINING

A wardrobe filled with fabulous frocks is only as desirable as the hangers used to display them. Transform your clothing collection without breaking the bank by jazzing up your hangers to make your clothes look more appealing. It's a good excuse to rummage through and re-discover all those garments you forgot you owned that have fallen at the back. Don't believe the theory? Give it a go.

Designed by Emma Watson

TOP TIP:
Take your time when using the varnish. Do not be tempted to overload your brush, as too much varnish can create small pools of discolouration when hung up to dry.

MAKE IT:

1 Start by removing any sticky labels and residue that may be on the hanger and then cover the metal hook with masking tape.

2 Spray paint the whole surface with metallic spray the same colour as the glitter you are using.

3 Apply PVA glue along one side of the hanger and sprinkle with glitter. Leave to dry, then shake off the excess.

4 Repeat step three on the reverse side of the hanger.

5 Use dabs of PVA and glitter to fill in any areas that were missed and leave to dry.

6 Carefully varnish all over using a small brush to seal the glitter and hang up to dry overnight.

CRAFT STASH:
* Wooden coat hanger
* Metallic spray paint (silver)
* PVA glue
* Clear gloss varnish
* Small paintbrush
* Masking tape

GLITTER:
* Glitter Flakes (silver)

GLITTER 101+

Use the same technique to glitter up other wooden objects like frames and boxes or old ornaments.

HOME SWEET (EARRING) HOME

TOP TIP:
Instead of using confetti glue, create your own by mixing small confetti style sequins in with any glitter glue, seal the design with varnish as before.

Crafty types are good at taking an object and figuring out alternative uses for it... never let it be said that a mug stand is only for hanging your tea cups. They also make fabulous jewellery stands. Hook on your earrings, bangles and anklets; having them on show also makes it easier next time you're accessorising an outfit and wondering what combination will work.

MAKE IT:

1. Paint the entire mug stand and leave to dry, add a second coat if required.

2. Go over it with a layer of confetti glitter glue.

3. Press each piece of confetti down to ensure it holds and that they are evenly spread out.

4. Finish by sealing in the design with a coat of clear varnish.

CRAFT STASH:

* Wooden mug stand
* Acrylic paint (pink)
* Brushes
* PVA glue
* Clear varnish

GLITTER:

* Flower Confetti Glitter Glue (Pink)

GLITTER 101+

Using confetti glitter in crafts is a great way to keep children occupied. Stir it in with poster paints for a quick DIY project that young ones will love such as making shimmery hand prints on large sheets of paper.

KITCHEN CALLING

Give in to your snack cravings...no one's looking!

CRAFT STASH:

* Kitchen jars (ensure they have a smooth base, these ones are plain silver metal)
* Ruler
* Pencil
* Tube of 3D paint

GLITTER:

* Self-adhesive glitter vinyl
* Tube of glitter glue

TOP TIP: Start applying the vinyl strips on the main section and rim from the back so that they begin and end in the same place.

GLITTER 101+

Recreate similar designs on plastic tubs and make people jealous when they see you out and about, eating homemade sandwiches.

MAKE IT:

1 Measure the width and length of the tin and cut out a piece of vinyl in your main background colour. The sheets are A4/8.5x11in in size so if that does not stretch across the length, you may need to cut more than one piece. As it is shiny the joins will not show, though it is best to put the joins at the back of the tin. Do the same with the rim of the lid.

2 Draw around the lid and cut out a circle of vinyl in your chosen colour. Peel off the backing and smooth into place ensuring there are no air bubbles.

3 For the rim and main piece, peel the corner of the vinyl. Position it, then use a ruler to smooth out the bubbles as you pull the backing paper away, leaving the vinyl adhered to the tin. It is permanent and difficult to reposition so keep an eye on it to make sure it is applied straight.

4 To finish, draw a speech bubble shape on the vinyl and stick in the centre of your tin. Use 3D paint to write a word in the middle.

FUNKY DAYS ARE BACK AGAIN

Make an ecological version of a groovy lava lamp, swapping electricity and a light bulb for salt and a torch. It's the perfect activity for children to make at a sleep over party, keeping them amused for hours (even after the lights have gone out.)

TOP TIP:
Swap a spoon of salt for a fizzing effervescent tablet for even more bubbles but make sure they are used supervised. Try washing salts, soap powder and bath salts to create different effects.

CRAFT STASH:
* Plastic bottle with a top
* Food colouring
* Vegetable or cooking oil
* Water
* Salt
* Spoon
* Torch

GLITTER:
* Leaf

MAKE IT:

1. Fill your bottle two quarters with water, stir in a few drops of your chosen food colouring, fix the lid on top and give it a good shake.

2. Top up the water with oil, filling the bottle another third so that it contains three quarters of liquid. The two sections will separate immediately.

3. Pour in a spoon of glitter and again, place the lid back on and give the mixture a good shake.

4. To create lava lamp style bubbles, add in a spoon of salt and watch it effervesce as it dissolves. Shine a torch on it to recreate an authentic lamp effect.

GLITTER 101+

Draw bubble shapes, like those created by lava lamps onto a canvas. Paint each section in a bright colour then apply glitter of the same shade on top to create a piece of retro art. Seal with an adhesive spray before hanging.

IS IT A BIRD? IS IT A PLANE? IT'S SUPERMAN!

Although I'm a Batman girl at heart, there's something very seductive about the strong graphic colours of red, yellow and blue in his costume that makes Superman so very appealing. Flick through any of his, or indeed any other comic, and you will notice the immense detail that goes into each illustration. Display these artistic talents in your crafts by using the pages for paper decoupage. Wait until you've finished reading the story of course!

CRAFT STASH:
* Canvas lampshade
* A comic
* PVA glue
* Paintbrush
* Fabric trim
* Scissors
* Fine tip applicator
* Glue gun

GLITTER:
* Ultrafine (holographic red)

MAKE IT:

1 Tear out pages of the comic and cut out your favourite scenes, images and phrases.

2 Use the brush to apply glue on the back of each piece, ensuring it reaches all the edges and smooth it in place onto the lampshade. Repeat with all the other pieces, at times lining them beside each other or overlapping them so there is complete coverage. Rather than folding them over the top and bottom edges of the lampshade, make sure the pieces line up at the ends so there is no need to fold them.

3 Paint over the whole lampshade with PVA glue and leave to dry.

4 Pick one prominent colour that appears in the comic (red) and using the fine tip applicator apply glue every time that colour appears on the lamp. Apply glitter of the same colour over the glue and shake off the excess.

5 To complete, affix a trim around the bottom in the same colour, using a glue gun.

TOP TIP:
To make sure you do not cover your favourite images, do a rough ordering of the pieces you have cut out, otherwise you may end up gluing all your favourite ones first then hiding them when it comes to overlapping gaps at the end.

GLITTER 101+

Make small lanterns using glittery paper, join with string and hang to instantly create a simple living room decoration.

The comic used for this design is Superman: The Adventures of Nightwing and Flamebird, DC Comics (2009)

Fabric decoupage is just as lovely as using paper. Turn to page 115 to see how to transform a plastic tray or bowl with your favourite cotton prints.

LEVEL PEGGING

Transform laundry pegs into objects of desire and give them a new job while you are at it.

CRAFT STASH:

* Wooden pegs
* PVA glue
* Novelty plastic buttons
* Acrylic paints in the same colour as the glitter
* Paintbrushes
* Ribbon

GLITTER:

* Fine

MAKE IT:

1. Paint each of your pegs. You will be able to paint three sides and the inside before leaving it to dry and turning it over to do the remaining side.

2. Coat the three sides, this time in a thin layer of PVA. Pour on your glitter, shake off the excess and leave to dry before repeating on the fourth side.

3. Finish by gluing novelty plastic buttons over them randomly.

4. To hang photos up, anchor the ribbon at each end and then use the pegs to display photos, pictures and inspiration in a line.

TOP TIP:

Pegs have plenty of uses other than hanging clothes out to dry and displaying photos. Pop a magnet on the back to display reminders on your fridge or use them to keep food packages securely closed.

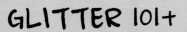

GLITTER 101+

Make wooden spoon puppets in the same way. Paint and glitter the entire spoon. Add googly eyes, draw features onto the main face and start sharing stories; a range of coloured puppets may be required for a full tale.

WILD THING

Frame your holiday snaps inside a miniature jungle.

CRAFT STASH:

* Frame
  (wood/papier-maché)
* Selection of plastic animals
  and a tree
* Acrylic paint (blue)
* Fine tip applicator
* PVA glue
* Glue gun
* Paintbrush

GLITTER:

* Fine in various colours to
  match the animals

TOP TIP:
Take the inside
of the frame out
before you paint it
to keep it clean.

MAKE IT:

1 Paint the frame in acrylic paint, leave to dry and apply a second coat if required.

2 Take each animal and highlight their skin with PVA glue such as the giraffe's spots, lion's mane and tiger's stripes. Then sprinkle glitter on, shake off and leave to dry. Do the same to a plastic tree. Placing the glue inside a fine tip applicator make sit easier to apply small details.

3 When they are completely dry use a dry brush to remove any excess glitter that may have collected in the grooves of the plastic animals.

4 Affix them onto the frame using a glue gun.

How to spy animals in the wild:
* Dress in camouflage so you aren't easily visible
* Pack a pair of binoculars
* Keep, very, very still (and quiet!)
* Learn to speak in an animal tongue and arrange a meeting with the leader of the pack

GLITTER 101+

Experiment with a disposable camera. Apply a small amount of clear or pale nail varnish and a few specs of glitter right on the lens, then snap away. It creates an unpredictable but beautiful effect, especially with translucent glitter and plenty of sunshine.

97

POT LUCK

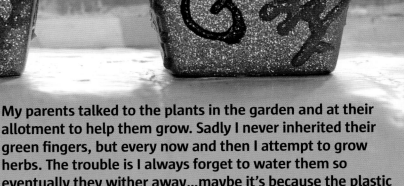

TOP TIP:
Write the name of what you are growing on the pot using glitter tubes so you can keep an eye on their progress.

CRAFT STASH:

* Ceramic plant pot with a wide rim
* Masking tape
* Measuring tape
* Glue gun
* Newsprint/scrap paper

GLITTER:

* Spray (gold and silver)
* Multi-surface 3D glitter tubes

GLITTER 101+

Spray your garden furniture with glitter to match your plant pots

My parents talked to the plants in the garden and at their allotment to help them grow. Sadly I never inherited their green fingers, but every now and then I attempt to grow herbs. The trouble is I always forget to water them so eventually they wither away...maybe it's because the plastic pots they are sold in are so boring that I forget they are there? The eye-catching sparkle of these pots should help.

MAKE IT:

1 Cover the rim of the plant pot with masking tape then turn it upside down. Place on paper and take outside.

2 Spray all sides of the pot and allow to dry. It is best to spray several thin layers in one go. The glitter paint will look runny and may leave 'running' marks on the pot but these will not show up when dry. Spray on another coat and allow to dry.

3 Turn the pot the right way up and mask off the open end. Spray it for a third time. This will give you a good coverage while allowing you to

appreciate the ceramic underneath. If you want a heavier finish, spray on more coats until you are happy.

4 When it is completely dry decorate the surface with the multi-surface glitter tubes. Write on a word or add foliage details. It is best to work freehand as these paints are free flowing, although you can sketch on your design with a pencil if you prefer. They can come out thick so practise on scrap paper first. Leave to dry fully (these paints can take up to 72 hours to dry so be patient!)

5 Finally glue on a strip of measuring tape on the rim before filling with compost and the seeds of your favourite bloom.

SHE SELLS SEASHELLS (AND STARFISH) ON THE SEASHORE

Make a mermaid feel at home in your bathroom when she lays eyes on this treasure from the deep...

MAKE IT:

1. Begin by coating both sides of the starfish with a layer of glitter varnish (allow the top to dry before working on the reverse) and then randomly sprinkle on a microfine glitter for added shimmer and leave to dry.

2. Using a strong glue and a paintbrush, add pearls and beads in the centre of the starfish and on the ridges to create a magical, mythical looking sea creature.

CRAFT STASH:

* A dried starfish or starfish ornament (this one was bought from Whitstable, a quaint English seaside resort)
* Selection of beads and pearls
* Strong glue
* Paintbrush

GLITTER:
* Gloss/varnish
* Microfine

GLITTER 101+

Decorate seashells in the same way and place along your bathroom windowsill to make you feel like you are living by the sea.

SEASONAL SNOWFLAKES

Christmas wouldn't be the same without glitter! As it's the season to sparkle, make sure your home is filled with glistening decorations like these pretty embroidered tree ornaments set inside mini embroidery hoops.

Designed by Kirsty Neale

MAKE IT:

1. Iron the felt and cut out a circle roughly 20cm/8in in diameter.

2. Draw around the inner section of your embroidery hoop, the one that does not have a screw at the top onto another piece of felt and cut out.

3. Transfer the snowflake template onto your first piece of felt, positioning it roughly in the centre. You can do this using dressmaker's carbon or by placing the design on a light box and tracing over it with a water-soluble pen.

4. Stretch the large piece of felt over your hoop and tighten the screw so it is held firmly in place.

5. Stitch over the design, using three to four strands of embroidery floss. Work the end sections in a detached chain (lazy daisy) stitch, and add French knots, as marked on the template. Use single, long stitches for the remaining details, working from the centre out when you make the six longest sections of the snowflake.

6. When you have finished stitching, take the felt out of the hoop and use a clean, damp sponge to remove any pen or carbon marks. Press gently and set aside to dry.

7. Take the outside part of your embroidery hoop and spread glue around the outer edges.

8. Working over a large piece of scrap paper, sprinkle glitter all over the glue. Shake off any excess, and hang the hoop over a door handle to dry.

9. When the hoop is dry, add a second coat of glue over the first layer of glitter, and repeat the previous step.

10. When the second coat of glitter is completely dry, place the fabric back in the hoop, making sure the stitched design is centred. Tighten the screw to secure. Glue the smaller circle on the back of the frame to hide the backs of the stitching on the main piece.

11. Cut a length of embroidery thread and work a line of loose running stitches (sew in and out in a straight line) into the excess felt at the back, around 3-4cm/1.2-1.6in from the outer edge of the hoop.

12. Pull the thread taut to gather the felt, and knot to hold in place. Trim any excess felt in the centre.

13. Take the circle of felt you cut in step two and spread glue over one side. Press down firmly over the back of the hoop to cover the gathered felt edges and hide the back of your stitching.

14. Tie a length of ribbon at the top of the hoop, where the fastening is, into a small, neat bow.

15. Cut a length of baker's twine or embroidery thread, and use a needle to slide it through the knot at the back of your bow. Knot the twine ends together.

16. Slip the twine under the screw in your embroidery hoop and pull upwards, so the bow sits neatly in place at the front. You can then use the twine to hang your finished decoration on the Christmas tree.

CRAFT STASH:

* 10cm/4in wooden embroidery hoop
* Felt, in colour of your choice
* Iron and ironing board
* Scissors
* Pencil
* Dressmaker's carbon, a water-soluble fabric pen or light box
* Embroidery floss (white, cream or silver/metallic)
* Needle
* Small, clean sponge or cloth
* PVA glue
* Small brush
* Scrap paper
* Ribbon (approx. 1cm/.5in wide)
* Baker's twine (optional)

GLITTER:

* German glass glitter (silver)

Template page 208

TOP TIP:
As an eco-friendly alternative to store-bought felt, why not try recycling an old sweater? Pick one which has a 90-100% wool content (either an unwanted woolly from your own wardrobe or a thrift-store find), run it through a hot, 90 C/190 F cycle in your washing machine and you should be left with a fully-felted sweater that is ready to cut up and use.

TOP TIP:
Try re-sizing the template and using a larger hoop to make a stitched alternative to a Christmas wreath. Hang it on a well-sheltered front door, or just inside your hallway.

GLITTER 101+

Make your own Christmas baubles. Spread glue over the glass part of a spent lightbulb, then dip in glitter. Apply a second coat and when dry wrap wire around the metal part of the bulb to create a loop or hook for hanging.

LET THERE BE LIGHT

It's not like you need an excuse to eat baked beans, but just in case you have to justify a second helping, here's how. Empty food cans are needed to make these recycled candle holders to hang from trees and the more lanterns you have, the better the atmosphere created at your garden party. So anyone for a third helping?

TOP TIP:
If you're wondering why you need to use a frozen can, it helps to maintain its shape while you are creating the holes.

CRAFT STASH:

* Empty food can (washed with label removed)
* Hammer
* Nails
* Marker pen
* Water
* Freezer
* Wire and wire cutters
* Candles (night/tea lights)
* Beads (optional)

GLITTER:

* Spray

MAKE IT:

1. Using your pen, mark two holes: one on either side at the top of the can. This is where the wire will be placed to hang the lantern.

2. Draw on your design by marking small dots all over the can. You could draw spots, swirls, shapes, words or repeat patterns, as long as they consist of dots.

3. Fill the can with water and freeze over night.

4. Place the frozen can on a table and hold a nail over one of your holes and hammer it in. It will go through creating a hole. Then move the nail around and punch holes in the same way at every dot.

5. When complete, wait for the ice to melt or pour hot water inside to speed it up.

6. Spray the outside of the can all over with glitter spray. Apply a second and third layer if you want heavier coverage.

7. When dry, cut a length of wire (as long as you want the hang to be) and feed it through one of the top holes, bend it over itself to secure. If you want to make a beaded handle, thread beads on now.

8. Secure the other end of the handle by bending the wire through it.

9. Place lit candles inside and hang and admire.

GLITTER 101+

Create wind chime sounds by hanging glitter sprayed cutlery all over your garden or above windows.

TIN ART

Sometimes I buy tins because they look nice; it doesn't matter what's inside. If they contain delicious biscuits it's a bonus. But what to do with them when the cookies are gone and there's nothing more than a few crumbs at the bottom? They are far too charming to throw away! Answer: place them on your kitchen windowsill and fill with utensils. It's much easier having them to hand than rummaging through your drawers trying to find a potato masher when you're in a hurry.

MAKE IT:

This project has no rules! The idea is to embellish already pretty tins with additional sparkle. Rather than hiding tins (the sort you get biscuits and sweets in or find empty at antique fairs) away, display them somewhere prominent by giving them a use like this. It also beats having to buy a boring metal utensil pot. Look at the shapes, lettering, patterns and motifs and add glitter to highlight them. The great thing about using a fine tip applicator is that it is easy to draw details and apply tiny shapes like dots. Go to town with the shimmer as much or as little as you like. Apply one to two colours at a time then shake off the excess. It will dry quickly so you do not need to wait too long before applying the next colour. When dry, your tins are ready for their new duty. You can also keep using them as tins so do not throw the lids away. Just be sure to give them a sprinkle of the sparkly stuff too.

CRAFT STASH:
* Vintage tins
* PVA glue
* Fine Tip Applicator

GLITTER:
* Fine and ultrafine in a range of colours to match the tins

GLITTER 101+

Draw designs on unusually shaped bottles with PVA glue in a fine tip applicator and add ultrafine glitter to instantly create original vases.

HEAVEN SENT

Working with Angelina fibres introduces you to a whole new sparkly world. Consisting of highly shimmering strands that are heat-bondable, they can be ironed together to create sheets of glitter that can be cut up and used in paper crafting, or used sparingly to add areas of sparkle to all types of textile and jewellery projects.

TOP TIP:
There is no wastage caused by Angelina fibres, any parts that you cut off or that fall off can be saved up and used again.

CRAFT STASH:
* Glass vase
* PVA glue
* Iron
* Greaseproof paper/ baking parchment
* Scissors

GLITTER:
* Angelina Fibres
* Leaf/chunky glitter

GLITTER 101+

Create sheets of Angelina fibre in different colours, trim them down to an A4 size, place in a laminating wallet and put through a laminator to create intricate, iridescent placemats.

MAKE IT:

1. Cut your greaseproof paper into two equal size sheets approximately A4/ 8.5x11in and pre-heat the iron to a medium setting.

2. When you open up the pack of Angelina Fibres you will notice they look like a bundle, yet they actually come apart easily. Simply ease off fibres and the place them on one of the sheets of greaseproof paper. Once you have created a layer, you can start adding extra fibres from different shades to build up areas of colour. At this stage you can also sprinkle glitter randomly on the fibres. They will mostly fall through the gaps so the more densely you layer your fibres the more they will catch the sparkle.

3. When you are happy with the quantity, cover the fibres with the second sheet of greaseproof paper then iron over it. The fibres will bond immediately creating a glittery lace like paper. At most you will be ironing for approximately 10 seconds.

4. You can continue to increase the size of your piece into a larger fabric by joining it to more fibres, just make sure each time that they are covered by the paper otherwise the fibres will melt onto your iron.

5. Hold your new fabric against the vase and wrap it around to check the fit – if it needs to be bigger simply join extra fibres on with the iron until you have a sheet that is large enough to cover the whole vase.

6. Paint a thick later of PVA glue on one side of the vase at a time then smooth on the fibre sheet, pulling it taut when you get to the edges. Also keep smoothing it out so there are no air bubbles and the fibres are fully fixed to the glass.

7. Add a further layer of PVA on top so when it dries, it will have a glossy finish.

8. Trim off any long pieces of fibre or leave these hanging if you want additional texture. Remember to keep all spare strands for next time.

MASTER IT!
Turn to page 24 to find out more about working with Angelina fibres

STEP BACK IN TIME

Vintage has long been a buzzword among fashionistas yet it is also a trend that has captured the artistry of the crafting community. Vintage is a celebration of the past capturing the look and feel of days gone by. Collectors should keep their eyes open for objects with a 'post war' aesthetic about them, like worn paint, faded, subdued colours and the use of fabrics such as lace and crochet. Images of historic characters evoking nostalgia like the decoupage papers used for this decorative plate are a popular design feature. As an inexpensive alternative to a traditional hanging, try covering your walls with ceramic plates as a clever way to introduce vintage style into your home.

Designed by Claire Barone

CRAFT STASH:

* Side plate
* Mod Podge
* Collage sheets (Debrina Pratt)
* Plate disc
* Small paintbrush
* Medium paintbrush
* Ribbon

GLITTER:

* Glaze
* Glitter glue pen

MAKE IT:

1. Cut out your chosen collage images, arrange on the plate and play around with ideas.

2. Take each image and apply one coat of Mod Podge with a small clean brush. Then position on the plate and use a medium size clean brush to press out any air bubbles. Continue until the whole design is complete. Leave the plate to dry.

3. Apply the glitter glaze over the plate with an even coverage and highlight any details with the glue pen. Add dots.

4. When the plate is completely dry apply one final coat of Mod Podge to the whole plate to seal and protect it.

5. Apply the plate disc to the back of the plate. Tie some pretty ribbon around the metal hook to make a knot or bow. Hang up.

TOP TIP: Source vintage plates in secondhand shops to give your final design an authentic look.

GLITTER 101+

Invite your friends over for a glitter plate swap. Ask them to bring over an old plate they don't need, decoupage as above, then pick names out of a hat to see who gets to keep which design.

To try out fabric decoupage idea turn to page 26.

CHIME OF YOUR LIFE

Drift off to the land of nod along to the soft jingle jangling of bells; guaranteed to give you sweet dreams. And that's not the only great thing about this project. It has two uses; doubling up as windchime and dreamcatcher...now you don't see one of those every day!

CRAFT STASH:

* Plastic or wooden bangles (6)
* Wooden dowel
* Small craft bells
* Seed beads
* Needle
* Screw eyes (extra small brass)
* Acrylic paint (pink)
* PVA glue

GLITTER:

* Standard (pink)
* Yarn (blue and pink)

MAKE IT:

1. Wind yarn around each bangle so that the entire surface is covered. To do this, cut a long length of yarn, tie it to the bangle and then wind it round and round until you come to the end. If required, tie on a second piece to complete the coverage.

2. To make the beaded chains, tie double threaded string to one end of a bangle and then thread on seed beads, using your needle. Add on a bell in amongst the beads. When you get to the end, tie it onto the opposite end of the bangle. Add as many beaded strands as you like.

3. Prepare the hanger by inserting screw eyes at the top, evenly spaced apart and then two at the bottom. They can be pushed straight into the dowel with your hand.

4. Paint the dowel with acrylic paint and when dry cover in a layer of PVA glue, then sprinkle with glitter.

5. To attach the bangles, cut two equal lengths of yarn (fairly long) and tie a knot at the end. Twist them together until you get to the end then pull the middle so the yarns double up as a cord and tie the loose end. Feed these cords through the bangles to hang them loosely together allowing them to move freely. The top two will be hung through the screw eyes in the hanger. Create a cord in a similar way to hang the chime/dream catcher up.

Do dream catchers really catch your dreams?

Some native American communities believe that if you hang a dream catcher by your bed, only good dreams will filter through while the bad ones can't get through. Others say that nightmares pass out of them and through the windows.

GLITTER 101+

Sprinkle loose glitter on the windowsill on days the tooth fairy comes to visit.

GIFTS & FOOD

A TOAST...

When it comes to wedding gifts, a pair of champagne flutes may be one of the most popular gift choices, but ask yourself, could anyone else's be as desirable as these? Absolutely not!

CRAFT STASH:
* Champagne flutes
* Glass paints
* Brushes
* Paper

GLITTER:
* Outline stickers

MAKE IT:

1 Paint the bottom of the glass first. Glass paint is thicker than ordinary paint in consistency but is more transparent so you will need to apply several coats to get a good coverage. Let each layer dry before adding the next.

2 Turn the glass upside onto a sheet of paper. Paint the main section of the glass as before. If you do not turn it upside down, the paint will run to the bottom.

3 When the glass is completely dry, smooth on outline stickers to create intricate patterns that look like Moroccan tea glasses.

TOP TIP:
You can also use glass-painting outline stickers that act as stencils. You place the stickers onto your glass, paint inside them, then when dry, peel off the stickers revealing your design underneath – a quick and effective way to get a result without the need to draw and transfer designs.

GLITTER 101+

Use glitter outline stickers to decorate the lid on your laptop and the backs of mobile phones.

TOP TIP:
This design is not permanent but will last a few washes when cleaned by hand, so warn the receiver they should only be used for special occasions (though they must be put on display the rest of the time!)

ANIMAL ATTRACTION

I once spent six hours on a safari trying to locate a leopard. Everyone could see the 'spot' apart from me; my eyes just couldn't hone in on her camouflaged skin against the wilderness. If on the other hand, she had been covered in sparkles, maybe, just maybe, I would have been the first to notice her? This project is dedicated to that Sri Lankan leopard.

MAKE IT:

1 Lay the initial down and paint all the sides that are visible using acrylic paint. When it is dry, check whether it needs any further coats as you need thick coverage, if so, keep applying then turn over and repeat on the side that was face down.

2 To create the animal print motifs use the thin black marker to draw rounded oblong shapes as shown. Then add borders and blobs to them randomly, colour these in with your marker.

3 Dab glue inside the shapes and sprinkle on the brown glitter.

TOP TIP:
Initials can be hung on doors to identify rooms, or spell out a whole name: a stylish way to brighten up a baby's nursery.

CRAFT STASH:
* Papier-maché initial
* Acrylic paint (orange)
* Black marker pens (thin and thick)
* PVA glue
* Paintbrush

GLITTER:
* Hexagonal (brown)

Try out these other animal skin designs using a similar technique:
* Snake lines
* Tiger stripes
* Giraffe shapes
* Fish scales
* Dalmatian spots

GLITTER 101+

Draw murals on nursery walls using ordinary paint then go over sections using a glitter glaze.

FABRIC STORY

If you're anything like me, when you step inside a fabric store you can't come out empty handed. Gorgeous cotton printed fabrics are so hard to say no to, even if you don't know what to do with them. It's worth buying a sample as you never know when you'll see something like it again. I bought this floral print fabric from a market stall when I was on holiday in Turkey and the elephant cotton was a gift from a friend visiting Australia. A great way to show off these textile treasures is through fabric decoupage: a technique that can be used to brighten up all sorts of objects and furniture.

CRAFT STASH:
* Plastic tray/bowl
* Cotton fabric of your choice (in two designs)
* Pinking shears
* PVA glue
* Water
* Brush

GLITTER:
* Varnish/Glaze

Want to try your hand at paper decoupage? Turn to page 94 to see how to make a comic book themed lampshade and page 106 for a decorative vintage plate.

GLITTER 101+

Brush glitter glaze onto doorknobs and door handles to make entering a room, so much more exciting.

MAKE IT:

1. Cut your fabric into squares of a similar size using pinking shears. These are scissors that create a zigzag edge to prevent fabric from fraying. To keep them sharp do not use them for anything other than material no matter how tempting it is!

2. Coat your whole tray/bowl in a layer of watered down PVA glue, approximately one part water to three parts PVA is good.

3. Carefully smooth your fabric pieces on alternately to create a patchwork effect. Allow the fabric to overlap the edge of the tray/bowl without gluing them down.

4. If there are any corners of fabric sticking up, apply glue on the underside and smooth down. Leave to dry.

5. Trim the edges of any fabric that is overlapping the edge of the tray/bowl.

6. Carefully varnish it with a coat of glitter gloss and leave to dry.

BATH TIME BLISS

Pencil in some 'me time' and lock the bathroom door behind you! These rich and indulgent bath bombs are the perfect gift to yourself; especially after a long week.

Designed by Brittany De Staedtler

TOP TIP:
This recipe is easily doubled or tripled because you are always using the same percentages so make as large a batch as you want.

BEAUTY KIT:

* 1 Part citric acid
* 2 Parts sodium bicarbonate
* Witch hazel
* Cosmetic safe colouring
* Fragrance or essential oil
* Olive oil
* Dome shaped mould
* Bowl and spoon
* Squirty bottle

GLITTER:

* Cosmetic glitter

For more spa crafting ideas turn to page 142 (soaps) and 134 (milk bath)

GLITTER 101+

Blend cosmetic glitter with a body oil or body gel and smooth onto damp skin for a post-bath moisturiser that will make your skin shimmer, before heading out for a night on the town.

MAKE IT:

1 Place the citric acid and sodium bicarbonate in a bowl and blend, blend, blend it up! This step is super important, as if you do not blend these ingredients well enough, you will end up with a grainy bomb. If you are making a large batch, you could do this in a blender.

2 Once blending is complete, add the colorant and glitter.

3 Next add fragrance oils to your personal preference.

4 Fill the squirty bottle with witch hazel and spray on the mixture while stirring with the other hand.

The mixture is ready to place inside the mould once it starts to stick together – time is of the essence. If you wait too long, the mixture will get hard. If you spritz too much, the mixture will be too wet and the fizzing reaction will start.

5 Once the moulds are filled, wait a few minutes and tap them out. Let them air dry for three to four hours until completely hardened.

6 To use, drop into a hot bath, lie back and enjoy the effervescing, shimmering, scented bath bomb explosion.

PUCKER UP

The perfect party season pout requires a seductive shimmer and thankfully it can be yours without the need to buy expensive beauty products. Follow this simple recipe using natural ingredients for killer, kissable lips.

Designed by Helen Hammond

TOP TIP:
Make several in different colours of the rainbow; one to suit every mood!

BEAUTY KIT:
* Rollerball bottle
* Sweet almond oil
* Glycerine
* Food colouring
* Food flavouring
* Small funnel

GLITTER:
* Cosmetic glitter with stars

MAKE IT:

1. Add one teaspoon of glycerine into a bowl and follow with one or two drops of food colouring and a small dash of flavouring.

2. Blend in a light sprinkling of cosmetic glitter and mix well.

3. Using a funnel, pour the lipgloss into a rollerball bottle then top with sweet almond oil.

4. Click the rollerball top into place and smooth onto your lips before heading out to party.

GLITTER 101+

Dip the tips of just-polished nails in fine glitter for a sparkly take on the classic French manicure.

DISCO DIVA

Going clubbing? Don't leave home without a pot of this dazzling body glitter!

Designed by Helen Hammond

GLITTER 101+

Stir cosmetic glitter into creams or lotion for sparkling beauty products.

MAKE IT:

1. Place the aloe vera gel into a bowl and sprinkle on your preferred glitter colours; be sparing for now.

2. Test the gel on your arm to see if you want to add more glitter to the formula. Add more if required.

3. Scoop a little from the pot and glide across your shoulders, arms, cheekbones and wherever else you want your skin to sparkle (avoid the eyes). Make sure it is fully absorbed for a professional looking shimmery finish.

BEAUTY KIT:
* Aloe Vera Gel
* Food Colouring (optional)

GLITTER:
* Cosmetic glitter (gold and green)

SHAKE IT UP!

Glitter is amazing! Group it together and you get a shimmering mass yet separate the particles and you can appreciate the beauty of each individual speck. By trapping it between transparent acetate you can shake up it, move it around and even observe the sound of it, which is a bit like gentle rain.

MAKE IT:

Pencil case

1. Make the heart fastening by tracing the template onto the felt and cutting it out. Cut a piece of acetate slightly bigger than the heart. Place holographic glitter and confetti glitter in the centre of it and place the acetate on top. Stitch around the heart to secure the glitter then trim off the excess acetate.

2. Line up two sheets of acetate and stitch a straight stitch on your sewing machine around three sides, leaving a 1cm/1/2in seam allowance. On the fourth side do the same but sew only three quarters of the way so that there is a large enough gap to pour in the glitter. Pour your loose hexagonal glitter inside. Sew up the gap.

3. Hold the sheet vertically and fold the top inwards 7cm/2.75in in from the top edge. Then make a second fold, directly in the middle of the rest of the sheet and fold it in. You will end up with a pouch consisting of three sections.

4. To make the case sew a line over both ends of the main folded section.

5. Cut two squares of Velcro and stick one inside the top flap and one inside the main pouch so that it opens and closes.

6. Glue the heart in the centre to hide the Velcro.

CRAFT STASH:
* Acetate
* Thread
* Felt
* Scissors
* Velcro/hook and loop tape (stick on)
* Sewing machine

GLITTER:
* Holographic (pink)
* Confetti (stars)
* Hexagonal

Templates page 199

TOP TIP:
Once you have stitched through acetate it will create holes. If you make a mistake and unpick the stitch then the acetate will be holey making it more difficult to use the same piece again - it's best to start with a new piece.

Phone protector

1. Make your heart in the same way as above.

2. Place your phone on a sheet of acetate and then fold it over so that it is sandwiched between with some room all the way around so that it can slide in and out easily. Cut two pieces of acetate this size.

3. Line them up together and fold in half, one side will not need any stitching as it is on a fold. Stitch up two sides and pour glitter into the third side before closing it up. Glue your heart in the centre.

GLITTER 101+
Stitch glitter inside larger acetate sheets and create book and passport covers in a similar way.

Snack alert:
Spoon me into small pasty
cases and make mini chilli
jam tarts.

KITCHEN CUPBOARD:
* 150g/ 5.3oz long red chillis,
  fresh, deseeded and
  roughly chopped
* 200g/ 7oz red bell peppers,
  cored, deseeded and
  roughly chopped
* 1kg/2.2lbs jam sugar
* 600ml/2.5 cups red wine
  vinegar

EQUIPMENT:
* Food processor
* Wooden spoon
* Plastic jam funnel
* Stainless steel Maslin pan
  with handle
* 6 x 250ml/1/2 pint pickle
  or sealable jars

GLITTER:
* 1/2 tsp Edible glitter (gold)

(Makes approximately 1.5
litres/1.6 quarts of jam)

CHEF'S TIP:
To test the setting of the
jam, remove the pan from the
heat and place a little jam on
a saucer. Allow it to cool then
punch a finger on top. If the
jam wrinkles it has reached
the setting point. If there is no
evidence of wrinkling, put the
jam back on the heat and boil
for another minute and then
test again.

GLITTER 101+

Make a rainbow jelly by stirring
edible glitter into packet a jelly
mix. Layer up different colours
in a clear dish, making sure each
layer is set before adding the
next for a party piece that
truly wows your guests.

JAMMY DEAL

Chilli Glitter Jam...who would have thought such a concept would work? This is as simple to make as it is surprising to eat and goes perfectly with everything from chapattis to chips. In fact, it's one of those preserves that crosses over the jam barrier and could quite comfortably fall into the sweet or savoury relish territory. The sparkling flecks of glitter suspended in the rich red jelly make an impressive gift, or if you're not sure your friends will like it hot, substitute strawberries for the chillis.

Recipe by Manju Malhi

COOK IT:

1. Place the chillis and red peppers in a food processor and blitz until they become a red pulp.

2. Put the sugar and the vinegar in the pan and cook on a low heat.

3. Scrape the chilli pepper mixture out of the bowl and add to the pan.

4. Bring to the boil and continue to boil for 10-12 minutes.

5. Take the pan off the heat, stir in the glitter and allow it cool. Test the setting of the jam.

6. After about half an hour, the glitter flecks will looks more evenly spread out in the jam. Ladle it into sterilised jars.

7. Seal tightly.

CHEF'S TIP:

Jars that are not sterilised properly could spoil the jam. To sterilise, heat your oven no higher than 350 F/180 C/Gas 4. The jars may crack if the temperature goes above that. Place two layers of newspaper on each shelf. Do not place newspapers on the floor of the oven. Then space the jars out on the shelves. Shut the oven door and sterilise the jars for about 15-20 minutes. Remove the jars from the oven and place on a heatproof mat.

SWEET LIKE CHOCOLATE

Couture chocolate is normally reserved for extra special occasions because of the price tag, which isn't very fair. Luckily these temptingly tasty truffles are made of just three simple ingredients that can be bought with the smallest of pocket money so get ready to give in to your chocoholic cravings whenever they strike.

Recipe by Jolekha Shasha

KITCHEN CUPBOARD:

* 200g/7oz Plain chocolate of at least 70% solids (can be substituted for 250g/8.8oz Milk chocolate or 250g/8.8oz white chocolate)
* 150ml/.3 Pints double cream
* A few drops vanilla extract
* Icing sugar (optional)

EQUIPMENT:

* Saucepan
* Bowl
* Teaspoon
* Wooden spoon
* Tray
* Greaseproof paper/ baking parchment

GLITTER:

* Edible sparkles and glitter in a choice of colours

(Makes approximately 25 truffles)

COOK IT:

1. Break the chocolate into small pieces and set aside.

2. Place the cream in a saucepan and bring to a gentle boil. Take the pan off the heat and immediately add the chocolate pieces to the warm cream. Stir well with a wooden spoon until all the chocolate has melted.

3. Pour the chocolate and cream mixture into a bowl and leave to cool down.

4. Take teaspoonfuls of it and gently roll between your fingers to form a truffle shape. (You might find it easier to dust your hands in a little icing sugar before you do this).

5. Place on a lined tray and leave to set for about 20 minutes.

6. Sprinkle them gently with the edible sparkles or glitter of your choice.

GLITTER 101+

Dip the bottom of soft fruits like grapes and strawberries into melted chocolate then sprinkle on edible glitter. Leave to set by standing them up on cocktail sticks to create elegant crystallized canapés.

CHEF'S TIP:
Place the individual truffles inside petit four cases, pop these inside a tissue-lined box, tie with a ribbon and give to a loved one for a heavenly homemade present.

123

CRUNCH TIME

KITCHEN CUPBOARD:

* 175g/6.2oz Unsalted butter (softened)
* 150g/5.3oz Golden caster sugar
* 1 tsp Vanilla extract
* 2 Eggs (medium, beaten)
* 400g/14oz Plain flour, sifted
* 1 tsp baking powder
* Royal icing mix (you will need to make a batch of a soft consistency for the piping work and a batch of a more runny consistency to coat the cookies)
* Food colouring of your choice

EQUIPMENT:

* Cling film
* Icing bag
* Bowl
* Teaspoon/fine paintbrush
* Wooden spoon
* Rolling pin
* Tray
* Greaseproof paper/ baking parchment
* Cookie cutters
* Wire rack

GLITTER:

* Edible sparkles and glitter in your choice of colours

(Makes approximately 12 cookies)

These cookies are so daintily decorated they look too good to eat! Luckily the icing keeps them preserved for a while so as long as they are stored in an air-tight tin, they can be admired and enjoyed properly before being served as an after dinner petit four.

Recipe by Jolekha Shasha

COOK IT:

1. Pre-heat the oven to 180°C/350°F, grease and line two trays with greaseproof paper/baking parchment.

2. Beat the softened butter and caster sugar in a bowl until light and creamy.

3. Add the beaten eggs and vanilla extract and combine the mixture well.

4. Sift the flour and baking powder. Mix until you get a soft dough.

5. Wrap the dough in cling film and chill in the fridge for an hour.

6. Roll the dough out on a floured surface and cut out cookie shapes using your cutter. Place on the lined trays.

7. Bake for about 15 minutes or until the cookies are golden brown in colour.

8. Remove the cookies from the tray and leave to cool completely on a wire rack.

9. Once cooled the cookies can be iced. Stir food colouring into your icing first.

10. Pipe an outline onto each cookie with royal icing of a soft consistency, using an icing bag.

11. Fill the cookie outline with royal icing of a runnier consistency. Try using a small spoon or fine paintbrush to apply it.

12. Decorate as desired with glittery sprinkles.

GLITTER 101+

Next time you have guests over, sprinkle a touch of edible glitter over biscuits and cupcakes to make catching up over a cuppa into an experience they won't forget in a hurry. Don't be surprised if ask to come back again soon.

CHEF'S TIP:
You can use any basic cookie recipe or adapt this one for different flavours substituting the vanilla extract for lemon, rose or even lavender, and icing them in a matching colour.

COASTING ALONG

Cold winter nights have their benefits and one of them is hiding under a huge knitted jumper, wearing thick fluffy socks and savouring a piping hot mug of spicy tea. Of course you'll need somewhere to rest it while you tuck into the accompanying ginger bread, and these icy coasters are perfect.

Designed by Fatema Hossain

CRAFT STASH:

* Faux white leather material
* Large self-adhesive felt pads (furniture protector pads)
* Double-sided sticky tape
* Flat saucer
* Pencil

GLITTER:

* White Glitter
* Self-adhesive glittered lettering and decorative shapes (red)

Feeling brrrr?

Make a mug of warming chai; a sweet and spicy Indian tea. Boil a mixture of half water and milk with two tea bags or loose tea, a pinch of ground cinnamon and ginger, a bay leaf, clove and cardamom pod and two teaspoons of sugar. Turn down and simmer for two minutes then strain and drink.

GLITTER 101+

Personalise mugs by decorating them with glitter ceramic markers. Draw on designs or write words as you would with an ordinary pen then follow the manufacturer's instructions. Ceramics are usually placed in the oven once decorated to make the embellishment permanent so it won't wash off.

MAKE IT:

1 Draw a circle with a 9cm/3.5in diameter on the self-adhesive felt pad and on the faux leather fabric and cut them out.

2 Tape both circles together using double-sided tape, ensuring the edges are fully stuck down where they meet.

3 For the crystallised edge, wrap a piece of double-sided tape around the edges of the coaster and trim off any excess.

4 Roll it in a saucer of white glitter so that it sticks to the tape. Roll for a second time to fill in all the gaps, making sure no more glitter will adhere.

5 To finish, peel off the letters for the coaster design, arrange and stick them onto the faux white leather side.

CLOSE YOUR EYES AND MAKE A WISH

Despite what you may have read on page 8, glitter isn't really made inside factories, it's actually made by fairies. Of course you have to keep quiet about that because fairies usually shy away from the limelight and aren't interested in taking the credit. But you can help them on their mission to make the world a more sparkly place by making and carrying around your own special fairy dust.

MAKE IT:

1 Create a funnel with your card by folding it into a cone shape and taping it together, ensuring there is a suitable size hole that the glitter can fall through.

2 Hold the funnel at the top of your jar and then pour your chosen glitter in. Do not fill to the top; leave an air gap so the glitter can be shaken around.

3 For your own unique blend of fairy dust mix two colours together by pouring in your first colour as a thin layer, then alternating layers with another colour and giving it a good shake in between.

4 Attach the chain. (Make two because you will want one for yourself as well as giving it away!)

TOP TIP: You can also add in tiny sequins like stars or hearts for an even more magical touch.

How to use fairy dust:

Wear and carry fairy dust with you at all times so you can sprinkle it:

1. Over yourself when you are feeling down
2. Over someone else you see who looks sad
3. Inside a wishing well so your wishes are more likely to come true
4. To attract a fairy's attention if you need help
5. To create a secret path so you don't get lost
6. At a party on the dance floor
7. To make your picnics more appealing (for this you will need to carry edible glitter inside your jar!)
8. In an emergency when you need to craft on the go
9. To bring good luck and fortune to whoever you are with
10. To put a smile on a strangers face

CRAFT STASH:
* Glass jar pendant charm
* Silver or metal chain
* Small piece of card
* Sticky tape
* Scissors

GLITTER:
* Any glitter/s you choose

PLANET DINNER TIME!

Lay the table sci-fi style and dine like the stars using space age cosmic cutlery.

CRAFT STASH:

* Cutlery with rounded plastic handles
* Rolling pin
* Greaseproof paper/ baking parchment
* Clear varnish
* Knife
* Pencil
* Oven
* Oven tray
* Acrylic gems (optional)

GLITTER:

* Fimo Effects (or other soft polymer modelling clay with glitter)

MAKE IT:

1 Start with the base colour of your first piece of cutlery. Fimo is sold in a square shaped block that has ridges on it making it easy to break off. To cover one piece of cutlery you will need a quarter of a block. Warm it in your hands and roll it around until it softens then form a ball shape.

2 Place the ball on greaseproof paper and use the rolling pin to flatten it into a circle. Position the cutlery in the centre and fold the edges over, it does not need to overlap so cut off the excess. Then roll it between your palms so the Fimo is even all over, and the whole handle is covered. It works better if your cutlery is rounded at the ends to start with as this helps create a better shape.

3 Roll out a small piece of a second colour, form a short sausage shape and press it over the edge of where the Fimo ends on the handle; this gives the coloured edge. Smooth it around in your fingers to ensure there is a neat join. Do this to all your cutlery pieces so they are covered in a layer of Fimo and have an edge to them.

4 Decorate each piece of cutlery. To create designs, roll the Fimo out, draw motifs using your pencil then cut out the shapes using a knife. You will need to smooth the edges or use your fingers to shape the ends then position them onto the handle and press down so they hold. Avoid narrow edges and try to ensure most of the motif is flat. Some bits like the ring on the planet spoon can be left if they are thick enough not to break off.

5 You can roll small balls and press them in to create circles, combine colours to give a marbled effect and mix up glitter Fimo with the plain variety. Acrylic gemstones can also be used by simply pressing them in.

6 When your designs are complete, place them on greaseproof paper on a baking tray and follow the manufacturer's instructions. For Fimo the oven needs to be heated to 110°C/375°F and the clay is baked in a conventional kitchen oven for 30 minutes. Do not exceed the oven time as this discolours the clay.

7 Leave the pieces to cool down then apply a coat of varnish to seal in the design and give them a glossy finish.

8 The cutlery is safe to use and can be washed and used as normal... time to get the dinner on!

MASTER IT!
See page 25 for more information about how to use Fimo.

GLITTER 101+

Fold glitter particles into Play Doh, Plasticine and other re-usable modelling clays to make model making more fun.

TOP TIP:
Fimo has infinite uses. Here are some other things you can make with it:
1. Beads for jewellery
2. Fridge magnets
3. Door signs
4. Keyring charms
5. Decoration for picture frames, pens and vases
6. Coasters
7. Figurines
8. Plaques
9. Tealight holders
10. Dominoes

SUGAR AND SPICE

This is one of those vanilla fudge recipes that is so divine it's likely to become a family favourite that will be savoured by your ancestors for years to come. A classic fudge with a hit of spicy nutmeg to warm the vanilla flavour; once chopped up and sprinkled with glitter, it becomes the best sweet treat in the world.

Recipe by Manju Malhi

KITCHEN CUPBOARD:

* 300ml/1.27 Cups double cream
* 200g/7oz Sugar
* 80g/2.8oz Butter
* A generous pinch of grated nutmeg
* 1 tsp Littlepod Natural Vanilla Paste

EQUIPMENT:

* Wooden spoon
* Shallow baking dish
* Greaseproof paper/ baking parchment
* Heavy based saucepan
* Sugar thermometer
* Hand held whisk
* Sharp knife

GLITTER:

* 1/4 tsp edible

(Makes approximately 16 pieces)

COOK IT:

1. Grease the baking dish with a little butter then line it along the sides and base with greaseproof paper. The butter helps the paper stick to the sides.

2. Place the cream in the heavy based saucepan with the sugar, butter and nutmeg. Bring the mixture to a boil on a medium heat.

3. Lower the heat and allow the mixture to simmer for at least 15 minutes, stirring continuously, until the sugar thermometer registers 115°C/240°F. The mixture is now at the 'soft ball stage', which means it can easily be shaped.

4. Add the vanilla paste and mix. Beat the mixture with the whisk until it becomes thick and almost like treacle.

5. Pour into the baking dish and allow to cool.

6. Cover and place in the refrigerator for at least one hour until firm.

7. Cut into squares and sprinkle with glitter.

CHEF'S TIP:
You can add raisins and nuts such as almonds to the mixture for a different variety of fudge.

GLITTER 101+

Make a summer time knicker-bocker glory by piling different flavours of ice-cream into a tall glass, separated by layers of fruits, and sprinkle the top with edible glitter instead of the usual chopped nuts and cocoa. Don't forget to add a wafer and a flake!

HERE COME THE GIRLS

Hen-dos, birthday parties or divorce celebrations: whatever festivities you are enjoying, send out a message to the public...it's your night and no one is going to stop you having fun. Make a sash for every girl in the clan so you can spot each other and get ready for some serious laughs. (Don't forget to pack a camera!)

CRAFT STASH:

* Satin fabric (1.5m/5ft)
* Wide orange trim (3m/10ft)
* Sequin trim (3m/10ft)
* Felt scraps
* Fabric glue
* Pinking shears
* Sequin machine or hand needles and thread
* Iron on Hot Spots!
* Iron
* Pencil
* Dress making pins
* Greaseproof paper/ baking parchment

GLITTER:

* Craft foil
* Glitter glue (green)

Templates page 204

MAKE IT:

1 Cut a rectangle of satin that measures 12cm/4.7in wide and 150cm/5ft long using pinking shears to prevent the ends from fraying.

2 You need two lengths of wide trim, one for each edge of the satin piece. Pin these in place and then stitch over the inner edge on a sewing machine using a straight stitch.

3 With right sides facing fold your fabric in half leaving a 25mm/1in seam allowance and stitch the open ends together to form the sash.

4 Cut two lengths of sequin trim and glue these on either side using fabric glue. Do this slowly ensuring it is flattened and fully stuck down.

5 Take your sheet of glue dots and draw the outline of your letters on the back using the templates. The letters need to be drawn in reverse. Cut these out and position on the sash glue side down.

6 Iron over each letter, one at a time, on medium heat with an even pressure paying particular attention to the edges then leave to cool down.

7 Peel off the paper backing, glue dots will be left behind. Place your foil, colour side up on top of the dots then top with a sheet of greaseproof paper. Iron over the paper, keeping an eye on the foil underneath to ensure it doesn't pucker up or burn but adheres to the dots. Remove the paper and lift the foil off. Repeat this process for every letter.

8 To complete the design, use the template to make a cocktail glass from felt, glue it on and add details with glitter tube paint.

TOP TIP: To make it simpler, draw your letters on using glitter fabric paint.

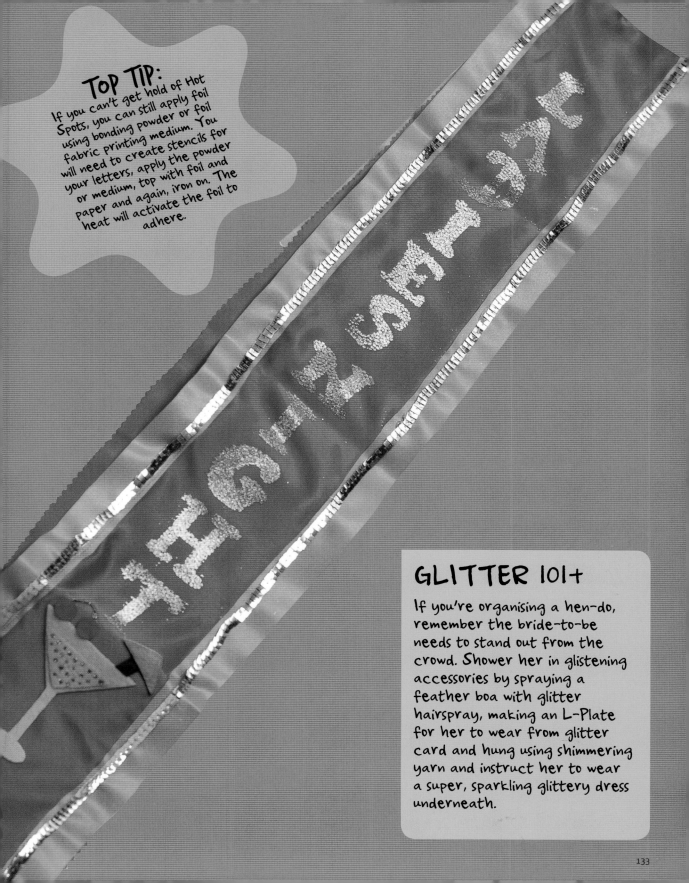

TOP TIP:
If you can't get hold of Hot Spots, you can still apply foil using bonding powder or foil fabric printing medium. You will need to create stencils for your letters, apply the powder or medium, top with foil and again, iron on. The heat will activate the foil to adhere.

GLITTER 101+

If you're organising a hen-do, remember the bride-to-be needs to stand out from the crowd. Shower her in glistening accessories by spraying a feather boa with glitter hairspray, making an L-Plate for her to wear from glitter card and hung using shimmering yarn and instruct her to wear a super, sparkling glittery dress underneath.

SMOOTH OPERATOR

Take a soak in luxurious waters filled with the cleansing and softening properties of milk and oats and let the flowers and sparkliness envelope you in a cloud of utter bliss. For added indulgence use roses, and emerge from the bathtub scented like a box of Turkish Delight.

BEAUTY KIT:

* Glass jar
* Powdered milk
* Oats (blended)
* Essential oil (rose)
* Dried flower (roses buds)
* Bowl
* Fork
* Spoon

GLITTER:

* Cosmetic glitter

MAKE IT:

1. Blend together two parts milk and one part oats (depending on the size of your container.)

2. Pour in a few drops of your chosen essential oil and mix it in.

3. Thoroughly stir in your glitter, adding as much sparkle as you want, and then pour the milk blend into your jar.

4. Top with dried flowers; rose buds work well.

5. Spoon into a hot running bath for a relaxing spa craft experience.

GLITTER 101+

Create striking eye make-up to rival Cleopatra's by blending Vaseline with cosmetic glitter for glistening eyeshadow. Apply to your lids, then outline with a thick line of black eyeliner and lashings of mascara.

Who was Cleopatra?
Cleopatra was the last queen of Ancient Egypt; considered the most beautiful woman in the land. Her secrets? Taking daily baths in milk and honey to keep her skin looking radiant.

TOP TIP:
Add your choice of essential oils to create the right mood for you. Lavender is perfect for unwinding before bedtime, while zesty citrus scents will revive your mornings.

DINNER IS SERVED

Hosting dinners, around your pad: every one is at it these days! But while most guests expect to be wined and dined as though they were in a Michelin starred joint, most will not expect to see snazzy napkin holders; now there's a topic to get the conversation flowing.

TOP TIP:
Take your time when you're peeling off the backing as the fabric can move and end up wonky.

CRAFT STASH:
* Plain napkin rings
* Magnetic alphabet letters
* Glue gun
* Double-sided tape

GLITTER:
* Fabric
  (Peacock mix by Josy Rose)

MAKE IT:

1. Measure the width and length of your napkin ring and cut a rectangle of fabric the same size.

2. Add strips of double-sided tape on the back, peel off, stick one end to the bottom of the ring then pull the fabric taught around the ring until both sides meet, making sure it is smooth.

3. Glue on the initials of each of your guests' names so they know where they are sitting.

4. Place your napkins inside and get serving!

Add even more personalised touches to your dinner party by making hand-stitched place cards, see page 180 for how to make them.

GLITTER 101+

Whether you're serving cocktails or mocktails between courses, sprinkle them with a touch of edible glitter for guaranteed oohs and aahs throughout the night.

MY FAIR LADY

Based on the colourful, intricate fabric parasols found in the Rajasthan region of India, this pimped-up wedding umbrella transforms from a dainty shade into a striking exotic ornament.

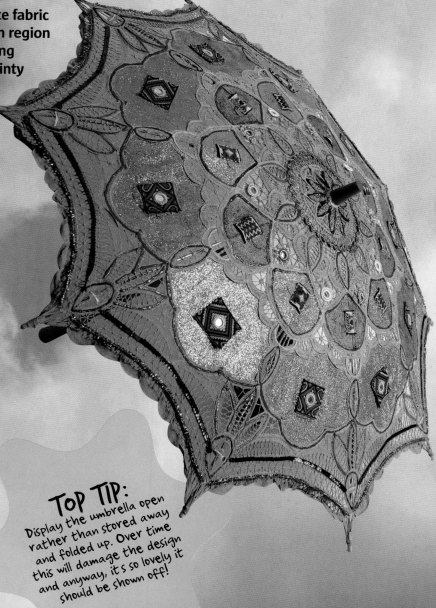

CRAFT STASH:
* Fabric parasol
* Shisha mirrors/small embroidery mirrors
* Fabric and sequin trims
* Glue gun
* 3D fabric tube paints

GLITTER:
* Assorted glitter glues

MAKE IT:

This is another one of those brilliant projects where there are no steps or stages to follow, just go with your instinct and glitter away.

These ideas may inspire you:

❋ Glue Indian shisha mirrors onto the flat areas (not on folds)

❋ Outline curves and shapes with fabric tube paint

❋ Spread glitter glue out to cover large sections

❋ Cut up motifs from trims and glue these on

❋ Alternate different colours

TOP TIP:
Display the umbrella open rather than stored away and folded up. Over time this will damage the design and anyway, it's so lovely it should be shown off!

GLITTER 101+

Brighten up a rainy day by customising a plain plastic rain mac with glitter fabric tube paints and permanent marker pens.

137

WORTH THE WEIGHT

You can be forgiven for getting hypnotised after one glimpse of this mesmerising paperweight. It is simply too good to waste sitting on your desk to stop notes from flying away. Let your colleagues assume it's just another piece of stationery and keep its other secret use to yourself: a meditation rock. Cup it in your palms and take a few deep breaths whenever you need a moment of peace and calm.

CRAFT STASH:

* Gedeo (or other two-part epoxy resin kit)
* An oval mould
* Vaseline or petroleum jelly
* Letter beads
* Sandpaper
* Measuring jug

GLITTER:

* All types in complimenting shades - fine, hexagonal, tinsel and confetti

MAKE IT:

1 Four layers of resin make up this design. The idea is to build it up with different types of glitter to create a coloured effect. You can add resin dye for colour, but this method shows how you can get just as good a result without it.

2 First of all work out how big you want the paperweight to be by pouring water into the mould up to that point and using a measuring jug to work out how many millilitres/ounces of resin you will need to mix up. Split this by the number of layers. If the total capacity is 100ml/ 3.5 ounces then you need four lots of 25mls/.87 ounces to get even sized layers, or if you want some to be thinner than others, adjust the quantities accordingly.

3 As always when working with a mould and resin, the mould must be completely dry to begin with and lined with Vaseline to make the object easy to remove.

4 Be experimental. Start by placing letters in the centre, spelling out any words you want. Cover with glitter and your first layer of resin. Wait for it to dry before applying the next one. To be on the safe side, leave it for 24 hours before the next layer...yes that's right. This four-layered paperweight will take four days! But do not let that put you off. The results are spectacular!

5 Glitter sinks so use a paintbrush to push it to the sides to create the sparkling concentric circles, otherwise it will fall underneath and you will not see it.

6 Once the top layer, the base, is dry and removed, it will need a little sanding to make it smooth.

MASTER IT!
See page 28 for more information about how to use

GLITTER 101+

Sparkle up other office essentials. Cover your diary and notebooks in glittery paper so that no one else can steal them and keep glitter ink pens to hand for ticking off your to do lists.

CRAFTY HEALTH WARNING:
Working with resin is seriously addictive.
Need another fix? Turn to page 28
to see how to make your own mould and
page 40 for directions on how to make a
resin pendant.

TOP TIP:
Be cautious when positioning the
letters. They tend to have a letter
printed on each side of the bead
that is reversed or upside down on
the other side. Whatever you see
from the angle of looking into the
base may not be what is shown when
you pop it out of the mould so lift
it up and check from the bottom
before you leave it to set.

MAKE
A
WISH

SPLISH! SPLASH! SPLOSH!

Move over Donald, there's a new duck in town and she's quackers about her personal appearance!

Designed by Kathy Cano-Murillo

TOP TIP:
Make a whole ducky family in different shades and designs representing different members of your household.

CRAFT STASH:
* 1 Rubber duckie
* Low-grade sandpaper
* Craft paint (black)
* PVA glue
* Paintbrush
* Crystals
* Gloss (spray-on sealer)

GLITTER:
* Black

MAKE IT:

1. Use the sandpaper to sand all over the duck. This is to remove the manufacturer's coating so the surface will hold the paint.

2. Cover the duck with a coat of black craft paint and let it dry.

3. Next spread a layer of PVA craft glue over the duck, on top of the paint, and pour on the black glitter until it is fully covered and let it dry.

4. Add glue on the back of the crystals and position them to create eyes.

5. Accent with more glitter if desired and spray with a gloss sealer to finish.

Rubber duck regatta
All over the world, people race their rubber ducks along the river, often for charity events. The largest annual meeting takes place in Ohio, USA where over 100,000 ducks take part.

GLITTER 101+

Keep a pot of cosmetic glitter in your bathroom and sprinkle in your bath to make your bubbles sparkle.

UNDERWATER LOVE

No one can resist the enchanting vision of a snow globe being shaken and then watching the flakes fall from the sky and float to the bottom. This one doubles up, not only is it a boredom breaker captivating office workers on important deadlines and children fed up with homework, it's also an aquarium without the worries of having to feed and look after live pets.

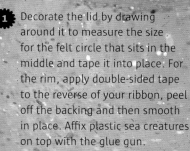

CRAFT STASH:

* Glass jar with a tightly screwing lid
* Water
* Plastic sea creatures
* Felt (green)
* Velvet trim
* Double-sided tape
* Spoon
* Glue gun

GLITTER:

* Holographic hexagonal in blue, green and white

MAKE IT:

1 Decorate the lid by drawing around it to measure the size for the felt circle that sits in the middle and tape it into place. For the rim, apply double-sided tape to the reverse of your ribbon, peel off the backing and then smooth in place. Affix plastic sea creatures on top with the glue gun.

2 Spoon glitter inside, in your choice of colours, holographic works well although you do not need a lot.

3 Fill up the jar with water. Fasten on the lid and shake it up!

TOP TIP:

Make jars with different themes for humorous house warming gifts. Add any kind of plastic toy, but not too many as they will end up as a heavy clump rather than floating objects.

Sea creature shock! Did you know, that jellyfish don't have brains!

GLITTER 101+

Fill clear plastic bottles with water, glitter and beads to make quirky shaker instruments that are perfect for jamming with at a music festival.

SOAP AND GLORY

When bars of soap are nearing their end, you get broken pieces that go slimy...instead of throwing them away, recycle them into brand new soaps with a touch of spa crafting.

BEAUTY KIT:

* Old pan
* Scraps of glycerin soap or melt and pour soap base
* Rubbing alcohol
* Spray bottle
* Fork
* Knife and chopping board
* Microwave and microwave proof bowl
* Mould
* Dried flowers, beads (optional)
* Essential oil (optional)
* Food colouring (optional)

GLITTER:

* Cosmetic glitter

MAKE IT:

1 Cut your soap base or soap scraps into small pieces and place in the microwave proof bowl. Heat at 15-second intervals and stir in-between until the base is completely melted and runny.

2 Quickly fold in fold in the glitter, essential oil and food colouring if you are using them to give the soap colour and fragrance.

3 Spray rubbing alcohol into the mould, this prevents the soap from bubbling up. Then pour the mixture into your mould. If any bubbles occur at the top, again spray some rubbing alcohol on them.

4 If you are using dried flowers arrange these on top of the mould.

5 Leave the soaps to set for a couple of hours then pop them out.

> Something smells good! For more spa crafting ideas turn to page 134 (milk bath) and 116 (bath bombs).

TOP TIP: Set plastic toys or beads inside the mould as you use it up they will come out in the bath.

GLITTER 101+

Sew shapes and words cut out from glitter felt onto your bath towels to customise them.

TOP TIP: Keep your soaps sealed in cling film to preserve them.

TOP TIP:
Create a soap-on-a-rope by filling small moulds half way and lining them up. Lay a piece of rope through the middle of them and then top up the mould with soap mix. When set they will be joined by the rope, which you can hang up in your shower room.

THE CASE IS CLOSED!

Keep important cards protected inside their own special holder that can be slipped inside a larger wallet, purse or pocket for safe-keeping.

Designed by Kirsty Neale

CRAFT STASH:

* Patterned fabric in two contrasting pieces
* Fusible interfacing (medium weight)
* Iron and ironing board
* Ruler or tape measure
* Scissors
* Sewing machine and/ or needle and thread
* Pins

GLITTER:

* Glitter glue in a shade to match outer fabric (red, pink and clear)
* Glitter elastic

Template page 209

GLITTER 101+

If you ever discover that your friend or colleague has the same dress, handbag or shoes as you, personalise yours with a touch of glitter glue so everyone knows you're the more stylish owner.

MAKE IT:

1. Iron fusible interfacing onto the outer patterned fabric for your case, and cut out a rectangle 14x15cm (5.5x6in).

2. Repeat with the contrasting inner fabric, cutting out a piece 10x15cm (4x 6in).

3. With right sides facing, sew the two pieces together along the sides and top (long) edge of the smaller piece.

4. Cut across the top corners (as indicated on the template), then turn out to the right side. Use the point of your scissors to carefully push out the corners for a neat, sharp finish. Iron flat.

5. Fold the lower side edges marked 'A' inwards, and turn up a narrow hem along the bottom edge, 'B'.

6. Stitch the bottom edge hem in place. Do not sew the folded side edges yet.

7. Fold the whole of the lower section up, along line 'C', matching side edges 'A' to side edges, 'D'. Pin to hold in place.

8. Stitch around the outer edges of the case, catching in the lower, folded edges and removing pins as you go.

9. Fold the case in half and iron firmly along the fold edge to crease. Add an extra line of stitching along the crease, again catching in the lower, folded section so you create two separate pockets for holding tickets.

10. Open the case out flat, and decorate the outside with glitter glue. Trace over lines and details and/or fill in small areas of the patterned fabric using the fine point of the tube or bottle. Allow to dry.

11. Cut a piece of glitter elastic long enough to wrap around the case, plus a 1.5cm/.5in overlap.

12. Position roughly a third of the way up from the bottom edge of the case, and place a button on top of the overlapped elastic ends.

13. Stitch through the buttonholes, both layers of elastic and the top (front) layer of fabric to fix the strap to the case. The elastic should keep your case neatly closed when it is not in use, but easily stretch and move out of the way when you want to open it.

TOP TIP: Adjust the pattern size to make a larger case for carrying lists, memos or even a passport and travel documents.

GANGSTER'S PARADISE

Live like a mermaid by hiding your treasures away inside a trinket box inspired by silky white beaches. Your pearls deserve it.

CRAFT STASH:

* Plain box (wooden or card)
* Acrylic paint (white)
* Shells
* Glue (PVA and strong)
* Toothpick
* Pearls
* Pearl coloured bugle beads
* Pearl coloured sequins
* Pearl paint or pearlescent glue

GLITTER:

* Fine iridescent
* Glitter varnish

MAKE IT:

Box

1 Paint all the sides and lid of your box white. It may need two to three coats for a good coverage, allow to dry between each layer before you paint the next one.

2 As a topcoat apply a layer of pearl coloured paint or pearlescent glue to create a shimmery finish. Again you may want to apply more than one coat.

Shells

1 Cover them with a layer of glitter varnish and leave to dry.

2 Using strong glue draw a line down the centre of each shell and position the pearls. As strong glues are tackier they will get to work more quickly to hold the pearls in place.

3 Apply a dusting of fine iridescent glitter between the pearls in case there are any gaps where glue may have spread out. You will find that as the glitter is so fine it will stick to ridges in the shell without the need to apply glue that will enhance the glittery varnish.

4 Add areas of bugle beads on the shells by painting on glue and pouring on the beads just as you would glitter and shaking off the excess. Pat them into place with a toothpick.

5 Glue the rims of each shell to stick them onto the lid.

6 To complete the box, add sections of PVA glue between the shells on the lid and pour on the pearl sequins. Again shake off excess and pat them to hold with the toothpick.

Turn to page 99 to see how to make a shimmering starfish to sparkle up your bathroom.

GLITTER 101+

Make a rainbow assortment of glittery shells by covering different sizes in PVA glue then covering each in a different colour until you have a complete spectrum.

ALL STOCKED UP

The bigger the stocking the more presents you should get. And that's why this one is so generously proportioned. Remember only good people get real gifts, the naughty ones get coal so when you're hanging it on your bedpost on Christmas Eve, be sure you say a few prayers first if you're worried.

MAKE IT:

1 Create a paper template of your stocking by drawing the outline of a giant sock. It should measure 50cm/20in in length, 20cm/8in across the top and at the bottom measure 25cm/10in at its widest point.

2 Fold your first piece of fur in half, pin on the template, draw around it and cut it out so that you have two stocking shapes. Do the same with the other colour so that you end up with four pieces.

3 Line up each cream piece with a red one (the cream is the outer and red the inner colour.) Turn the top over by 9cm/3.5in creating a red edge and pin them together 1cm/.4in in from the edge.

4 Sew these two sides together using a cream thread so that the stitch is invisible. (Leave the red collar for now.) You can either use a straight stitch on a sewing machine or do a running stitch by hand. The thickness of the fur should hide the stitches.

5 Switch to a red thread and stitch the collar down. You will now have two complete halves of the stocking that you need to pin together.

6 To join them, cut a length of red embroidery thread (as it is thicker than ordinary thread, you will need a wide eye needle.) Using a 'whip stitch' along the whole edge, remove the pins as you go. A whip stitch is where you sew across an edge. Each stitch measures about 1cm/.4in in length and there is a 1cm/.4in gap between them. It is easier to do the stitch at a slight angle from each other.

7 For the Matryoshka doll motif, copy several versions of the template as you will need to cut it up to complete the design. First draw around the main body and cut it from felt. This is the base the rest of the design will be affixed to.

8 To attach each section iron on a piece of paper-backed fusible webbing onto the back of the fabric you are using. Cut the section from the template, draw around it on the paper and cut it out. Peel off the paper, position it on the main body and then iron it on so it fixes. Do this for each part of the costume.

9 The face is made from a circle of felt, use the template as a guide to create the hair and add features with eyes and tiny red pom-poms. When the doll is complete, glue it in the centre of the stocking.

10 Finish the decoration by gluing on glittery pom-poms at random.

11 Cut a 30cm/12in length of ribbon, fold it in half and stitch the ends together. Then feed inside the left corner of the stocking, about 5cm down and stitch it in place. Your stocking is now ready to hang up and fill with goodies!

CRAFT STASH:
* Faux fur in red and cream (1/2m/20in each colour)
* Felt and scrap fabrics
* Paper backed iron on fusible webbing (Heat n Bond Ultra Hold)
* Thread (to match fur)
* Small googly eyes
* Small pom-poms (red)
* Ribbon
* Paper
* Needles (hand and wide eye)
* Scissors
* Dressmaking pins
* Iron
* Fabric glue (optional)
* Sewing machine (optional)

GLITTER:
* Embroidery thread (red)
* Pom-poms

Template page 206

What is a Matryoshka?
A Russian nesting doll. They are normally made from wood and consist of a set of dolls that fit inside each other, getting smaller each time. The intricate designs and costumes worn by them are based on cultural dress and folk paintings.

GLITTER 101+

Don't forget to leave Santa a thank you note for the gifts. Write him a glittery message on glittery paper so he remembers to come back next year.

TOP TIP:
Follow the same pattern to make the stocking from felt. It is a great material for sewing projects as it does not fray, comes in endless colours and is perfect for appliqué work like the dolls outfit.

CARDS & PAPERCRAFT

HIPPY CHIC

Could recycling get more glamorous? From a distance no one will know those sparkly beads you are wearing were once in your rubbish pile. They glimmer like precious stones, only they are much more ethical! Hooray!

Designed by Fatema Hossain

MAKE IT:

1 Take the cover of a magazine that is about A4/8.5 x 11in in size. Mark lines on it, which are the width of the ruler and cut them out so you have five strips.

2 Fold the strips in half then roll them around a pencil tightly, but loosely enough so that you are able to roll them off again. Secure the end with a piece of sticky label.

3 Draw a triangle, with a base measuring 2cm/.8in and height of 26cm/10.25in.

4 Use this as a template. Lay it over a page from a magazine , you will be able to choose what you want at the end of your triangle. If you require specific words or colours make sure they are at the tip.

5 Apply the glue stick on the base area and the tip of the triangle then roll over one of the bases made earlier. Repeat for the other beads.

6 Coat them in PVA glue and roll them in glitter. Allow to dry, then roll the ends in more glue and glitter. Finish off with a glaze of glitter glue in a different colour.

7 Thread the beads onto stretch elastic and tie a knot. Measure the size of your wrist, but work with a greater length of elastic as it makes it easier to handle and to tie the knot. You can add more or fewer paper beads or include other beads to get the size and look you want.

8 Apply a dab of strong glue to the knot and trim the loose ends.

CRAFT STASH:

* Old magazine with a glossy cover
* PVA glue
* Small brush
* Stretch elastic 30cm/12in
* Beads (assorted)
* Strong glue
* Ruler (30 x 4cm/12 x 1.5in)
* Pencil
* Small strips of sticky label (use any white labels and cut them into strips of 1 x 4cm (.4 x 1.5in)
* Glue stick

GLITTER:

* Glitter varnish
* Glitter glues

TOP TIP:
Join beads together to make pendant shapes or make more beads for a necklace and earring set. Attach the bead to findings to make a whole range of recycled jewellery.

Glitter 101+

Give wooden beads a disco makeover with a coat of glittery varnish.

Eco Chic:
For more recycled fashion ideas, turn to page 42 to see how to transform an old bra into an evening bag.

'I'M DREAMING OF A WHITE CHRISTMAS'

Send snowy seasonal sentiments. The secret to this striking design is stamping onto acetate. A technique that looks utterly impressive but, sssssshhh, it's actually super easy!

Designed by Virginia Fox

CRAFT STASH:

* Starry paper (14.5 x 10.5 cm/ 5.7 x 4 in) (Space Stars from Craft Creations)
* White card (31.5 x 14.5 cm/ 12.4 x 5.7 in)
* Acetate (14.5 x 10.5 cm/ 5.7 x 4 in)
* Angel hair paper in white (14.5 x 5 cm/ 5.7 x 2 in)
* Rubber stamp (Tree Scene by Penny Black)
* Ink pads (black and white)
* Scrap white card
* Scrap blue mirror card
* Stamp cleaner or baby wipe
* Gelly pen (blue)
* Silicone glue
* Roller glue pen
* Pencil
* Ruler
* Embossing tool

GLITTER:

* Ultrafine (iridescent)

MAKE IT:

1 Ink the 'Tree scene' stamp with white and press the image twice on the acetate to form a line of trees about halfway up. Before the ink is dry, sprinkle with glitter and leave to dry completely before shaking off excess glitter.

2 Clean the stamp and ink it with black, then stamp the tree scene twice in the same position on the starry paper as you had done on the acetate. Leave to dry.

3 Lay the white card out horizontally. Working from left to right, score lines at 10.5cm/4in, 21cm/8.25in and 26.5cm/10.4in. Fold at each score line to form a card that, from the side, looks like two pyramids next to each other, one large and one small.

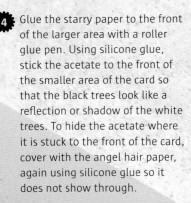

4 Glue the starry paper to the front of the larger area with a roller glue pen. Using silicone glue, stick the acetate to the front of the smaller area of the card so that the black trees look like a reflection or shadow of the white trees. To hide the acetate where it is stuck to the front of the card, cover with the angel hair paper, again using silicone glue so it does not show through.

5 Write a sentiment of your choice on scrap card with the gelly pen. Once dry, mount on a slightly larger piece of blue mirror card and attach to the front.

Glitter 101+

Pour glitter inside greeting cards and envelopes to surprise unsuspecting recipients.

TOP TIP:
Stamping ink holds glitter so is a brilliant way to make designs on transparent acetate that you can cut out and mount.

ppy Christmas

Other uses for glitter at Christmas:
* Sprinkle on doorsteps to welcome visitors
* Spray on an artificial Christmas tree
* Place inside presents so it falls out along with the gift
* Use edible glitter to liven up mince pies (after they have been warmed up!)
* Cover pinecones and branches in glitter and glue for instant table decorations
* Put on all your cards

BIRDS OF PARADISE

Whether you're stretched out on a sun lounger or sitting in front of your living room TV; cocktails and mocktails should be served up in the most exotic manner possible and sometimes sticking a kitsch umbrella into a cherry just doesn't cut it. Birds sitting in your glass on the other hand are ideal; the more flamboyant and striking the better.

CRAFT STASH:

* Wooden BBQ skewers
* Bird print or patterned paper
* Craft feathers
* Card
* Sparkling beads
* Scissors
* Fine tip applicator
* PVA glue
* Glue gun

GLITTER:

* Ultrafine in assorted colours (for umbrella)
* Rainbow shades (for stirrer)

The bird print wrapping paper used in these umbrellas is designed by Jill Green.

Template page 196

MAKE IT:

Umbrella

1. Cut a circle from your chosen paper with a diameter of 12cm/4.75in.

2. Using the fine tip applicator apply PVA glue to areas of the design you want to emphasise.

3. Add your chosen glitter, shake off and repeat with further colours until you have enough coverage.

4. When dry, cut a slit in the circle from one edge to the centre. Then form the umbrella shape by cupping it into a cone shape and gluing the end.

5. Push a skewer through the centre, add on your bead and top with a feather. The feather will push down through the hole so glue the end of it to the top of the skewer with the glue gun and also dab between the bead and where it meets the umbrella to ensure it holds.

Stirrer

1. Cut out a bird from card and cover one side with an even layer of PVA glue.

2. Visually split the bird into sections to work out where you want to stop and start each colour. Begin with the red on the head, pour on what you need then move straight to orange and keep going until you have created a rainbow bird. Leave to dry and repeat on the other side.

3. Glue a skewer in the centre and to hide it, cover in glue and glitter in the colour of the section it is in.

4. Finish by applying decorative feathers.

Glitter 101+

Wrap a strip of double-sided tape around your glasses before a party. Peel off the paper backing and sprinkle glitter over the sticky tape to decorate. When the party's over, peel the tape off and wash away any residue to return the glasses to normal. And of course don't forget to sprinkle edible glitter on top of all your tipples!

A recipe for the perfect summer mocktail:

Blend together 1 ripe mango, 1 ripe avocado, 1/2 banana, 1/2 glass of pineapple juice, 1/4 glass of coconut milk. Add crushed ice, a few fresh mint leaves and slice of lime to serve.

TOP TIP:

As well as rainbow glittering, try shaded glittering by working with colours that blend into each other like different vibrancies of blue. Start with a royal blue, follow with a medium blue then pale blue, before changing into green with a turquoise shade.

EAT ME!

A sparkly card and gift in one...what could be better?

Designed by Emily Burt

MAKE IT:

1 With your coloured paper held landscape, fold the two vertical sides in by 4cm/1 3/5in so that they meet in the middle.

2 Fold each side back towards the outside by 2cm/.8in.

3 Fold the horizontal bottom edge up by 2cm/.8in.

4 You now have the pocket that the edible glitter will go in to.

5 Turn it over and decorate the front using stickers, glitter, pens or stamps.

6 Place a 5cm/2in length of sticky tape on the back on each vertical edge and a 4cm/1.5in piece of tape along the bottom edge. Peel the backing off the tape and position the pocket on the front of your card.

7 Decant some edible glitter into a plastic bag. Write a label to go on the front of the bag so that the recipient knows they can eat the glitter!

8 Put the bag of glitter in the pocket, write a message inside and post.

CRAFT STASH:
* Card and envelope (C6 Size/4.5 x6.4in)
* Double-sided sticky tape
* Decorations (stickers, coloured pens and paper shapes)
* Coloured paper (16cm/ 6.33in by 11cm/4.33in)
* Scissors
* Small sealable plastic bag no bigger than 7cm/2.75in by 8cm/3.25in
* Label (smaller than the size of your plastic bag)

GLITTER:
* Edible

Glitter 101+

Start a mail art challenge among your friends. Send the first recipient a small blank sketchbook and sachet of glitter and ask them to decorate a page. Once they're done, they need to pass it on to someone else, who will fill up a different page with their own glitter art, before giving it to the next person. Write your address on the back of the book so whoever fills the last page will post it back to you.

SENDING OUT AN SOS

Receiving something with your name on is the most exciting part of getting post. So next time you sit down to send an email to a friend or realise you haven't texted them in a while, change your habits and send them a handwritten correspondence instead.

Designed by Kathy Cano-Murillo

TOP TIP:
Use the same technique to create matching writing paper to send with the envelopes; printing, colouring and glittering around the edges so your paper has a border.

CRAFT STASH:
* Envelopes
* Paper
* Assorted markers
* Black ink pad
* PVA glue
* Fine tip applicator
* Paintbrush
* Water
* Thick book
* Sticky label

GLITTER:
* Any standard glitter

MAKE IT:

1 Rub the ink pad all over the front of the envelope to give it a background texture and color.

2 Colour in a small sheet of paper using your markers. Take your paintbrush, dip it in water and use the marker drawings as watercolors. Rub a wet paintbrush to pick up colour and use it to accent the envelope.

3 When dry, place the envelope inside a thick book so it will flatten.

4 Use the glue inside a fine tip applicator to draw swirled designs and then pour on glitter. Tap away the excess and let it dry.

5 Pop a sticky label on the front so you can post it.

Glitter 101+

Write the inside of greeting cards using glitter marker pens or glitter tube paints to make your messages stand out.

WHEN YOU WISH UPON A STAR...

Warning: this is a magical wand that will make your dreams come true, so use it wisely!

CRAFT STASH:

* Wooden dowel, knitting needle or paintbrush
* Card
* PVA glue
* Strong glue or glue gun
* Satin ribbon (assorted colours)
* Double-sided tape
* Masking tape
* Streamers
* Collage materials of your choice (felt, scrap fabric, feathers, broken jewellery, gems)

GLITTER:

* Tinsel

Template page 199

TOP TIP:
Fairy wands can be made in any shape, not just stars. Other shapes that have magical powers include hearts, butterflies, hedgehogs and cupcakes...

MAKE IT:

1. Use the template to cut two card stars.

2. Take your handle (the dowel or substitute) place it in the middle of one star and draw a line to indicate where the stick will be visible from.

3. Lay out your ribbon and attach a strip of double-sided tape all along it (aim to get ribbon the same width as the tape). Pull away the end of one side of tape and affix it to the line you marked on the dowel.

4. Wind the ribbon downwards along the dowel, removing the backing of the double-sided tape as you go. You can keep it one colour or cut it off and wind on a second colour as in this design. When you get to the end, trim the ribbon and ensure the bottom is completely covered. Stick gems along if you like.

5. Tape the handle to the centre of one of your card stars using masking tape.

6. From the same spot, tape on streamers that will dangle down.

7. Cover the points of your second star with PVA glue, cover in a layer of tinsel glitter (which is two-tone so has an iridescent shimmer adding a fairy touch). Shake of the excess and leave to dry.

8. Decorate the front side of your star using collage materials of your choice. You could:

* Create concentric stars getting smaller and smaller towards the middle
* Add a patch
* Stick on a small toy or trinket
* Glue on broken jewellery
* Sprinkle on glitter in another shade
* Decorate with gemstones
* Write a word
* Create a 3D motif like the one here. To do this cut two leave shapes from felt and glue two smaller leaf shapes on to it in a satin fabric. Glue gemstones along the edge. Mount onto a feather base, glue a piece of broken jewellery in the middle and then affix it into the centre of the star.

9. When your collage star is dry attach it to the other star with strong glue or a glue gun.

Do you want to meet a fairy?

Turn to page 127 to see how to make your own fairy dust, which will help in your mission.

Glitter 101+

Make party streamers using glitter tissue paper, by cutting into equal size strips, taping them across a line of string and hanging from one end of your ceiling to the other.

WINGS OF DESIRE

Little butterflies will enjoy taking off in these 'so-cute-you-wish-you-were-younger' fairy wings. The template is child size, but there's nothing stopping you from enlarging them and making a pair for yourself.

Designed by Venus Muscat

MAKE IT:

1 Using the upper wing template, trace the wing shape onto card then flip over and repeat for the left hand side of the wing. Repeat with the lower wing template so you have a complete upper fairy wing and lower fairy wing.

2 Decorate. Cut out shapes from glitter felt or add swirly designs or lines with glue and sprinkle glitter on top. Just ensure both sides match up. Leave to dry.

3 Glue the upper wings onto the lower ones, checking the centres match.

4 Cut two pieces of ribbon approx. 75cm/30in long (or as long as you would like).

5 On the back of the fairy wings, glue the middle of each ribbon onto the middle of the connected wings in an X shape and leave to dry. These will be tied around the child's arms when wearing the fairy wings.

6 Cut a piece of glitter felt large enough to cover the front and back of the central join. Glue and leave to dry then get ready for take-off!

TOP TIP:
Use glittery card as your base for extra sparkly wings.

CRAFT STASH:
* Card (A1/33.1 x 23.4in size)
* PVA glue
* Double-sided satin ribbon (silver, 1.5m/5 ft)

GLITTER:
* Fine (purple, light copper, holographic silver)
* Glitter felt

Template page 202

Impressive butterfly facts:
* There are over 24,000 species of butterfly in the world (and 140,000 moths!)
* Some moths never eat anything as adults because they don't have mouths. They must live on the energy they stored as caterpillars.
* Butterflies have their skeletons on the outside of their bodies, called the exoskeleton, which protects it and keeps water inside their bodies so they don't dry out.
* Butterflies cannot fly if their body temperature is less than 30 C/86 F.

Glitter 101+
Sprinkle loose glitter onto the leaves of houseplants to make them shimmer in the sunlight.

FEELING FRUITY

Use these tempting stickers in your papercrafting, or post them around town on street furniture in a secret act of 'healthy' graffiti.

TOP TIP:

Double-sided adhesive film is like two large pieces of paper (A4/8.5 x 11in) stuck together that peel apart. They allow you to turn anything you want into a sticker. 3D foam stickers like these work really well and you don't have to do fruit. Make any sticker you want!

CRAFT STASH:

* Fruit stencils
* Funky foam/neoprene
* Double-sided adhesive film (A4 sheets/ 8.5 x 11in)
* Brush
* PVA glue
* Glue stick
* Pencil

GLITTER:

* Fine or ultrafine in assorted colours

Templates page 203

MAKE IT:

1 Trace the templates onto the foam. Choose a colour that best matches your fruit like yellow for the banana and red for the strawberry.

2 Glue these onto one side of the double-sided film which looks like an ordinary paper surface. When it is stuck, cut around the foam without leaving a white border.

3 Using a pencil, mark on the details for each fruit (leaves and spots.)

4 Paint PVA glue onto the first area you want to glitter, for example you may want to add sparkle to the branches of the cherries. Pour on the glitter, shake it off and leave to dry.

5 You can then apply the second area of glitter. You may want to create a completely glittery sticker such as the pear or just add some details like the lemon.

6 When the glitter is completely dry, peel off the backing from the reverse of the fruit and get ready for some serious sticking!

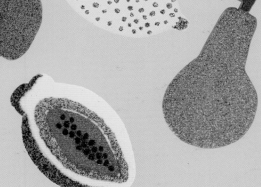

Glitter 101+

Sprinkle edible glitter onto a real fruit salad for a nutritious party snack.

STICKY SITUATION

Gone are the days when presents came wrapped up in transparent sticky tape. Glitter tape doubles up as a ribbon and be cut into shapes.

Designed by Shimelle Laine

MAKE IT:

1. Start by placing your glitter in something wide and shallow like a tray or if you do not have one, a large piece of paper.

2. Decide the length for your tape and cut that length from clear tape. Add a little to the measurement so you have a bit at the ends to make it easier to handle.

3. Press the sticky side of the tape onto the glitter, then pull it taut to release any extra sparkles back onto the tray. Repeat this until your entire length of tape (except the very ends) is evenly covered in glitter.

4. Use the tape to decorate parcels to create a sparkly ribbon effect. Add on any collage embellishments like a doily, tags and butterfies and use foam tape to make them look 3D.

5. To create glitter tape shapes, dip half the length of tape in glitter, then fold the tape in half, so all the glitter is stuck inside a tape sandwich. You can then cut the tape into shapes with a punch (like these butterflies) or scissors, and glue them on.

CRAFT STASH:

* Plain brown wrapping paper
* Craft papers and punches or die cuts to make the background motif
* Collage materials (small paper doily for gift and badge for notebook)
* Clear tape (sellotape, scotch tape, packing tape, etc)
* Foam tape
* Hot pink paper
* Hot pink adhesive rhinestone
* Adhesive gems
* Pen
* Paper or tray

GLITTER:

* Hot pink and turquoise

Thought of the day: Is it acceptable to wrap up a present and give it to yourself?

TOP TIP:

Often the cheapest stuff works best. Designer Shimelle tried the same technique with satin-finished office tape and then a cheap roll of non-branded sticky tape from a bargain shop, and the cheaper version had a better grip on the glitter and sparkled more!

Glitter 101+

Fold glitter tape into bows by cutting and joining several strips and stick on top of wrapped presents.

CROWNING GLORY

Only the finest jewels were worn by the Mughals who wouldn't leave their palaces unless they were kitted out in rubies, emeralds and diamonds. Luckily their fashionable ways were not buried with the rest of ancient Indian history. Modern maharajas and princesses from all lands can feel just as resplendent, in their very own headwear that is fit for royalty.

TOP TIP:
Look at images of Indian bridalwear where Mughal inspirations are a popular theme. You will get an idea of the placing of gemstones and patterns created by grouping colourful jewels together.

CRAFT STASH:
* Thick card
* Elastic
* Acrylic paint (pink)
* PVA glue
* Selection of acrylic gemstones in different colours and sizes
* Fine tip applicator
* Paintbrush
* Single-hole punch

GLITTER:
* Fine (various colours)

Template page 198

MAKE IT:

1. Use the template to cut out a crown and with the punch, create a hole at either end, 2cm/.8in up from the edges.

2. Paint the crown, leave to dry and add a second coat if required.

3. Use a glitter glue tube to create a fine line, all around the edges of the crown creating a border.

4. To make your crown sparkle enough to satisfy a Mughal princess, glue gemstones in lines over the crown. Larger gems will look like huge glistening rubies and smaller stones will give detail.

5. Outline the gems with a line of glue using the fine tip applicator, then sprinkle on your glitter and shake off excess. Do this to most of your gems, using a different colour of glitter each time for a more lavish effect.

6. You can use a dry paintbrush to rub away excess glitter that may have collected on the card.

7. When you are pleased with the final design, thread elastic through the holes.

Glitter 101+

Welcome guests into your own palace with a glittery doormat. Spray an ordinary straw matt with gold glitter spray and line the edges with gold sequin trim, glued around.

Interesting fact:
The author of this book Momtaz, is named after the Mughal Empress Mumtaz for whom the Taj Mahal, in Agra, India was built as a gift of ever-lasting love by her husband Shajahan, to remember her after she passed away.

GETTING INTO A PULP

Anyone with a love for craft will have a place in their heart for handmade paper. It's one of the most satisfying of recycled crafts and any paper goes. Be it old receipts, torn wrapping paper or a fast food leaflet, simply blend it up to make fresh sheets. I didn't try making it for years because I thought it involved owning expensive equipment, then I realised this is a myth. Papermaking is far less complicated and far more rewarding than it seems.

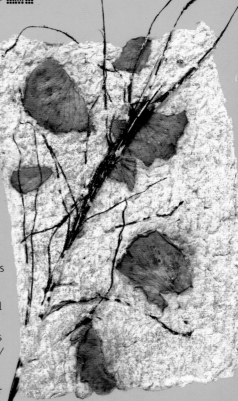

Beige: Magazine pages, fine gold glitter, dried petals and the stem of a peacock feather

CRAFT STASH:
* Wooden picture frame
* Gauze
* Masking tape
* Scissors
* Spoon
* Different types of scrap paper (like white, coloured, magazines, tissue)
* Collage items (optional)
* Felt
* Towel
* Blender
* Bowl

GLITTER:
* Experiment with different types!

MAKE IT:

1 Cut a piece of gauze that fits across the frame and tape it in place.

2 Tear your chosen papers into small pieces and place them inside the blender. Three A4/ 8.5x11in sheets worth will make enough for an A5/ 8.33x5.75in piece.

3 Pour warm water into the blender so it is two thirds full and blend the paper on high until a watery pulp is formed.

4 Pour the pulp into a bowl and mix in your chosen glitter.

5 Spoon the paper pulp onto the gauze frame filling up all the space. Spread it out as much as possible and flatten with the spoon to squeeze out access water.

6 Flip your frame onto a piece of felt, the paper should come straight off. If any is left behind on the gauze, scrape it of and spoon it onto the paper.

7 This is the stage where you can neaten the edges so if you want smooth ends, straighten them up or leave as they are for a jagged finish.

8 You can also press any collage materials in now and add a final sprinkling of glitter. The paper should be left to dry completely, this can take around three days, leaving it outside will make it dry faster. Your paper will peel away easily from the felt and then it's ready to use.

Blue stars: Blue sugar paper, blue shiny paper, gold foil glitter and gold and green star confetti

Blue sugar paper, green wrapping paper, blue glittery yarn, specs of angel fibres and ultrafine glitter

Some uses for handmade paper:

* Cut up for card making
* Make pages for a notebook
* Cover a book
* Frame as art
* Punch a hole at the top and join several to make a wall hanging

Pink: Light pink sugar paper and dark pink tissue paper and multicoloured hexagonal glitter

Glitter 101+

To add instant sparkle to your love letters, give writing paper a light spray of glitter hairspray before you start penning your thoughts. Before sending, add a quick spritz of perfume to mask the smell of the hairspray.

Green: Green printer paper and feathery green glitter

PAWS FOR THOUGHT

Keep your paws on your keys with this feline charm, or dangle from a suitcase so you can spot your luggage as it comes off the airport conveyor belt. After all, there's nothing more annoying than seeing a passenger carrying bags just like yours. With this attractive identification tag, that complication will be sorted!

Designed by Gemma Corner

TOP TIP: Instead of buying the kit, try making your own cat themed shapes from thick card.

CRAFT STASH:

* Maya Road chipboard keychain set (cat)
* Galeria Mineral texture gel
* Versamark Watermark stamp pad
* Embossing Powders (in colours of your choice – ranges by Heat it Up! and Moon Glow were used here in lilac, orange, coral, yellow, green, gold, plum, red and black)
* Heat embossing gun (A tiny hairdryer used for crafting)

GLITTER:

* Embossing powder

MAKE IT:

1. Apply Galeria Mineral texture gel to random areas of the chipboard pieces. Leave to dry then repeat on the reverse.

2. Cover one side of the word 'Cat' with Versamark Watermark ink and sprinkle several colours of embossing powder in random areas so that you achieve a camouflage effect. Tip off the excess powder.

3. Heat set the powder with a heat gun until it shimmers.

4. Again, apply Versamark Watermark ink over the whole of one side.

5. Cover the inked side with embossing powder and tip off the excess.

6. Heat set the side once again until it looks super glittery.

7. Repeat steps two to six with the remaining sides.

8. Repeat steps two to six with the remaining pieces. Varying the colours of embossing powder will make the final coat of embossing powder differently in the light.

9. Thread the chipboard pieces into ball chain and you are ready to lock up!

Glitter 101+

Make your luggage stand out from the crowd by customising your suitcase with glittery tube paints. Write the words of your favourite destinations or freehand doodle to your hearts content.

TRAVEL BUG

Sequin mesh looks like honeycomb and is a by-product of the sequin making process (the holes are left where the freshly cut sequins pop out). Rather handily, it acts as the perfect stencil, especially when it comes to glitter crafting.

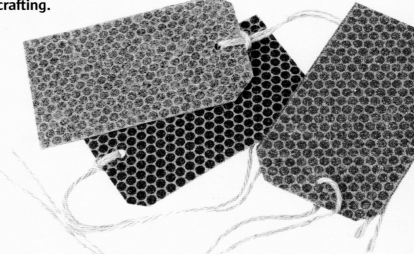

CRAFT STASH:
* Tag template
* Double-sided adhesive film
* Sticky label
* Single hole punch
* Sequin mesh
* Twine
* Scissors

GLITTER:
* Holographic gold and ultrafine (blue, pink and green)

Template page 201

Glitter 101+

Create a luggage tag by following the same instructions, writing your details on the back and getting it laminated. The only difference is that you punch the hole at the end.

MAKE IT:

1. Cut out a tag from the card using the template and then make one from the adhesive film.

2. Peel off one side of the film and smooth it onto the card.

3. Position your punch in the top middle of the tag about 1cm/.5in in and make a hole.

4. Peel off the top sheet of the film and place a piece of mesh on top flattening and smoothing it out so there are no bumps. You can lift it off and reposition if necessary.

5. Sprinkle on a coating of your main background glitter, shake it off, turn the tag upside down and peel off the mesh.

6. Place the glittered tag onto a clean surface and pour the gold holographic glitter over it which will stick to the gaps left behind by the mesh. Shake off the excess and leave to dry.

7. Wind twine through the hole so you can tie your tag and stick a label on the reverse to write your message.

TOP TIP
If you do not turn the tag upside down after the first colour, excess glitter will fall into the gaps; an effect you do not want.

BABY GA GA...

Sweet dreams are guaranteed when the little one catches a glimpse of this mesmerising mobile.

CRAFT STASH:
* Two wooden dowels (sanded at the edges and measuring 30cm/12in)
* Card (same shades as your glitters)
* Seed beads (same shades as your glitters)
* PVA glue
* Brush
* Glossy Accents
* String
* Needle
* Single-hole punch
* Pencil
* Screw eyes (extra small brass)

GLITTER:
* Tinsel (pink, blue, lemon and mint)

Template page 200

TOP TIP:
Don't stop at animals try space aliens, sea creatures or planes, trains and automobiles! One thing is for sure, new parents fed up with cuddly toys and yet more baby-grows will appreciate a handmade gift that occupies their little bundle of joy so they can sit back and enjoy a much-needed cuppa.

MAKE IT:

1. Use the template to cut each animal from card, you will be matching the glitter and the card up, so for green glitter use green card, blue glitter blue card etc.

2. Punch a hole near the top of the animal so that it can be hung.

3. Paint one side of each animal in a thin coat of PVA glue ensuring you cover all the way up to the edges. Lift the animal up and transfer it to a clean sheet of paper then sprinkle on a layer of glitter. As tinsel glitter has large particles it is unlikely you will need a second coat; having the same coloured card also helps. Shake off the excess then leave to dry.

4. Turn the animal over and do the same on the reverse, again move it to a clean sheet of paper when you apply the glitter.

5. Paint over one side of each animal with a layer of Glossy Accents and allow to dry before turning over and repeating on the reverse. Glossy Accents seals in the glitter leaving a three-dimensional shiny finish as though your work has been coated in plastic.

6. For the top level, draw two holes on the dowel 10cm/4in in from each end and twist in the screw eyes, you can do this by hand. Then thread a long piece of string with your needle and create a knot at the end. Place your seed beads on in alternate colours so you end up with a beaded chain and knot the end. Thread it through the screw eyes to create your hook so the mobile can be hung.

7. On the bottom of the dowel, mark two further holes 3cm/1.2in from the sides and fasten in the screw eyes. To hang each animal, again make a beaded chain, this time in the same colour as the glitter. Tie one end of your string through the hole in the animal and start beading from there. When you get to the top end, tie it to the screw eye. To hide where the chain meets the animal, cover the ends in PVA glue and a sprinkling of glitter. Repeat this on the second dowel so that all four animals are hanging.

8. To join the two dowels, make a mark in the bottom centre of the top one, and the top centre of the second dowel and affix screw eyes. Like the handle, create a multicoloured beaded chain and tie to both ends. Your mobile is now ready to hang up.

Glitter 101+

Apply a coat of glittery varnish to nursery furniture. Babies are fascinated by shininess and knowing they are living in a sparkly universe will make them feel relaxed, which equals fewer tears, and a happier mum and dad.

NEWSWORTHY NAILS

Have the news at your fingertips, quite literally!

CRAFT STASH:

* Newspaper
* Scissors
* Nail undercoat
* White nail varnish
* Rubbing alcohol (surgical spirit, available in chemists)
* Bowl

GLITTER:

* Nail varnish

MAKE IT:

1. Cut the newspaper into small rectangles just bigger than each of your nails.

2. Prepare your hands with a simple manicure, ensuring they are clean, trim, buffed and filed.

3. Paint each nail using the white nail varnish.

4. When dry, dip one nail in a bowl of rubbing alcohol, just for a few seconds, then take it out but do not dry it.

5. Take one of the newspaper pieces and place it text downwards onto your nail, ensuring the whole piece becomes wet. Smooth it out flat then lift it up, the text will have printed onto your nails.

6. Repeat this for each of your nails.

7. To finish, paint on a top coat with a clear glitter nail varnish to seal the design and add sparkle.

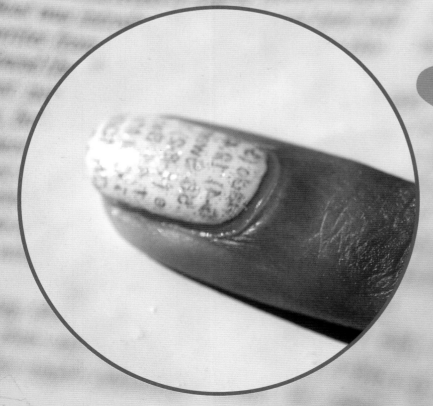

TOP TIP:
Use a nail varnish with a light coverage, not one that's densely glittered or it will hide the text.

Glitter 101+

Draw designs using eyelash glue on your skin and cover with cosmetic glitter for instant glistening temporary tattoos.

TOP TIP
The text will print in reverse, if you want it to face the right way, photocopy or scan and print the text in reverse so that when you apply it, it will transfer correctly.

GIVE NOTICE

Never forget a thing with this 'eggstremely' useful recycled memo board that once housed the main ingredient to make your morning omelette, and now reminds you of your daily 'To Do' list.

CRAFT STASH:

* Large egg box tray (or smaller egg boxes joined together)
* Acrylic paint
* Thick, coloured string
* Strong glue
* Strong tape

GLITTER:

* 3D tube paints
* Leaf
* Glitter glues
* Foam

MAKE IT:

1 Paint the egg tray with a coat of acrylic paint and repeat with a second layer if required.

2 Fill the inner grooves of the tray with 3D paint, alternating between two colours and then sprinke on some leaf glitter which will get caught in the paint.

3 Brush glitter glue onto the pointy tips of the tray, again alternating two colours.

4 Cut a rectangle of glitter foam and edge it with a line of 3D tube paint.

5 Write the words 'Notes' in the middle and glue to the top of the tray when dry.

6 To complete, tape a piece of coloured string at the back of your notice board so you can hang it up. You can now pin items onto the pointy glitter glue covered tips.

Glitter 101+

Create matching pins to use on your board by brushing the heads with a hi-tack glitter glue or painting them with PVA and a sprinkling of fine glitter.

CRAFT STASH:

* Card (2 x A4/ 8.5x11in sheets, blue)
* Honeycombed textured watercolour paper (2 x A4/ 8.5x11in sheets)
* Recycled paper (10 x A4/8.5x11in sheets, pastel blue)
* Paper (10 x A4/ 8.5x11in sheets, white)
* Lace paper (1 sheet)
* Ruler
* Bone folder
* Double-sided sticky tape
* Spray mount glue
* Mini bulldog clips or large paper clips (4)
* Book making awl
* Cutting matt
* Velvet ribbon
* Decorative beaded trim
* Bicone beads (44 that are 4mm/.15in and one at 5mm/.2in)
* Needle and linen thread

GLITTER:

* Glitter glues in a mixture of colours

Glitter 101+

Doodle in glitter by swapping your pencil or biro for a glitter glue pen to brighten up notebooks, sketchbooks or post-it notes.

WRITE STUFF

Two of anything is better than one. So reach for this handmade notebook with separate compartments when you need to scribble down several thoughts at once. Use one half for keeping a shopping list of the boring things you need to buy, like washing up liquid, and save the other half for the daydream items you wish you could treat yourself to, like a designer handbag. Just remember to turn to the right page when you hit the shops!

Designed by Fatema Hossain

TOP TIP:
Use a variety of papers inside like squared or tracing paper and use coloured embroidery thread instead of linen thread. You can also alter the sizes to make small books you can carry around in your purse or larger sketchbooks for displaying artwork.

MAKE IT:

1 Fold a sheet of blue card in half and run the bone folder down the side to make a crease. Repeat with the other sheet so that you have two covers. Then do the same with the honeycombed papers and place one inside each cover.

2 Lay five pale blue sheets and five white sheets alternately and crease the fold of each sheet as before. Place them inside. You will now have two booklets with cover sheets and mixed papers inside.

3 Open each one out and find the centre page. Hold the sheets and covers together using bulldog or paper clips at each end so they do not move. Then use a ruler and pencil to mark out 2.5cm/1in from the edge either side of the centre spine on each booklet. Mark a third spot in the centre. This will indicate where to make the holes for sewing the booklet together.

4 Place the books on a cutting mat then using a book-making awl, make a hole at the three dots. Do this for each booklet.

5 Thread the pages and the cover together with cream linen thread using a hand needle. Start by entering the needle and thread out through the middle hole, next thread on your small bicone beads and then go into the hole on the left side. Take the thread back out of the middle hole, thread on your beads and go into the hole on the right side. Then back to the middle and tie a secure knot in the middle of the booklet. Cut the thread off and use the bone folder to squash the thread down and into the hole to make it neater. You will now have a book with a beaded outer spine. Repeat for the second book.

6 Join the two booklets together with double-sided sticky tape.

7 Next take your lace sheet and cut two pieces to fit the front of your double joined notebook and one for the back. Spray glue, onto the back of them, then carefully affix to the blue covers.

8 Glaze the lace with a coat of glitter glue to add some sparkly details.

9 To finish, glue a strip of velvet trim to the front and back inner edges and then tie a tasselled cord around. Thread on four of the smaller bicone beads and the larger one so that they create a beaded motif in the centre of the spine where the two books meet, then tie it in a knot at the front, so no one can peek inside.

GLOBAL GATHERING

Bring Latin fever to your next party with a Mexican papier-mâché piñata filled with scrummy, yummy sweets and treats. The only down side is that to eat them, you will need to smash up your hard work first.

Designed by Fatema Hossain

MAKE IT:

Piñata

1. Blow up the balloon to a medium size and tie the end.

2. Tear newspaper up into random pieces.

3. Mix flour with water in a ratio of four spoons of flour for every one of water until it forms a runny paste. Add extra water if needed.

CRAFT STASH:

* Balloon
* Newspaper
* Flour
* Water
* Acrylic paint (red and yellow)
* Tissue paper (white)
* Cardboard
* Masking tape
* Double-sided sticky tape
* Cotton embroidery thread (orange and yellow)
* PVA glue
* Copper or other wire (14cm/5.5in)
* Disposable gloves
* White felt
* Thick white thread
* Roll of wrapping paper

GLITTER:

* Standard gold

Template page 206

4. Place the balloon on top of a container that can hold it while you work, like a plant or cooking pot. Wearing gloves, dip your fingers into the flour paste and coat the balloon. Lay the newspaper pieces randomly on top and overlapping each other. Once the first layer is covered add more paste to the surface and build up another one. Do not worry about smoothing the layers as ridges will add character and create an interesting effect when it comes to the painting stage.

5. Leave the balloon to dry for up to 36 hours.

6. Cut the top end of the balloon and squash down the base a little so that it can stand up. There will be an opening at the top to pour in your treats. By now the balloon will have dried out and burst, if not, you can prick it with a needle and then remove it.

Decorating

1. Paint the shell red then leave to dry before adding some yellow. Do not cover the red, just emphasise ridges and mix with red in places to get orange areas.

2. When dry, transfer the paisley template over the shell, in red. Paint the parallel red lines on, then add the white details.

3. Sparkle up the paisleys with gold glitter by painting on PVA glue, sprinkling the glitter on and shaking off the excess.

4. Cut a strip of white felt 10cm/4in wide and long enough to go around the neck of the balloon. Fold over the felt and stitch it in place to create a collared rim.

5. Make the handle by cutting a piece of cardboard into a 35cm/14in long and 5cm/2in wide rectangle and folding it in half. Cover it with tissue paper to create a padded handle and attach it to the inside of the shell with masking tape.

6. Coil the wire to make a circle and cover with masking tape to make your hanging loop. Attach to the handle using masking tape.

7. Wrap yellow embroidery thread around the handle creating a wrapped criss-cross effect. Dot PVA glue in between the lines and add gold glitter. Your piñata is now ready for filling, but to play, you need a stick!

Piñata stick

1. Take the roll of wrapping paper, fold the edge inwards and stick down with double-sided tape.

2. Cover the roll with white tissue paper and secure with a long strip of masking tape.

3. Tie red and yellow embroidery thread around the roll in a criss-cross fashion. Place glue dots randomly between some of the spaces and sprinkle on gold glitter to match the piñata handbag handle.

How to play with your pinata

Fill it with lightweight candies, glitter, stars, shreds of glittery paper and any other confetti you have.

Use the loop to hang the pinata from a tree branch or a nail hung above a doorway. Make sure everyone taking part is aware of the rules for hitting the pinata, which are that only one person hits the pinata at a time and everyone stands back and awaits their turn. Whoever breaks it gets to keep the goodies that fall out. Sharing them is optional!

THE TABLE IS SET

Home entertaining has never been so popular, but remember it's not just the food and company your guests will be rating. Every detail leaves an impression. These personalised, hand-stitched place cards are so thoughtful it won't matter if you burn the dinner.

Designed by Emily Burt

CRAFT STASH:

* Bird template
* White card (A4/ 8.5x11in)
* Cotton sewing thread
* PVA glue
* Coloured pens
* Scissors or craft knife
* Ruler, preferably metal
* Sticky tape
* Sewing machine

GLITTER:

* Glitter felt fabric

Template page 196

MAKE IT:

1 Cut an A4/ 8.5x11in piece of card in half so that you have two pieces measuring roughly 21x14.5cm/ 8.5 x 5.5in. This will make two place cards.

For each place card:

2 With the card held horizontally, measure 7cm/3in from the top and carefully score a line across using a ruler and blade of the scissors. Fold along this line. The bigger piece will be the front of your place card and the smaller piece will be the back.

3 Stitch an outline in a decorative stitch around the front edge of the place card. Pull the threads to the back of the card and secure with sticky tape.

4 Using the template, cut your bird shape out of glittery felt.

5 On the back of the bird shape, put a line of glue around the edge and place it on the front left of the place card inside the border.

6 Draw a speech bubble in coloured pen and write your guest's name inside.

Adam

ex

Glitter 101+

Make a dazzling table centre by spraying dried fruit and flowers with glitter spray, arranging them in a bowl and adding a drop of essential oil to create a homely welcome.

TABLE MANNERS

Laminated placemats are a cheap and easy way to make every dinner party you host seem different. Create a theme to suit your meal or interior and enjoy compliments about how original they are as your guests tuck in.

CRAFT STASH:

* Access to a laminator
* Laminating sheets
* Large sticky labels (A5/8.3x5.8in)
* Lace or paper doily
* Paper

GLITTER:

* Fine or ultrafine

MAKE IT:

1. Carefully peel the backing paper off the label and place it on a piece of paper, sticky side up, making sure it doesn't curl over at the ends.

2. Lay your choice of stencil (lace trim or doily) on top, and press and pat it down, making sure there are no bumps.

3. Pour glitter all over the label, immediately lift it up, and shake it off.

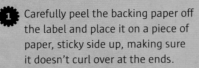
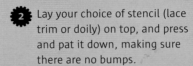
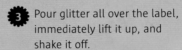

4 Hold the label upside down and peel away the stencil.

5 Place it inside your laminating sheet. These mats have been made by placing two A5/8.3x 5.8in size labels inside, you can get A4/8.5x11in labels but they are more difficult to manage as they are likely to curl up.

6 Turn on the laminator to heat it up and when you are ready, feed it through to set the design.

7 If you want to use two colours of glitter like the pink and turquoise example, pour a second colour on immediately after you have peeled the template off, glitter will adhere to the gaps.

Glitter 101+

Lace glittered papers are great for using as backgrounds in card making, so make a range of them that you can cut up and use for greeting cards.

GARDEN OF EDEN

Do you know someone who sneezes whenever they receive the real thing but desperately wants to own a bunch of flowers? Surprise them with a pop up card instead, it will result in just as big a smile and best of all, lasts longer. (Forever, if they keep the card safe!)

Designed by Virginia Fox

TOP TIP: Once you have made one pop up card you can use the technique to make endless variations.

CRAFT STASH:

* Card blank (10.5 x 21cm / 4 x 8.25 in)
* Purple paper (10.5 x 21cm / 4 x 8.25 in)
* Card (pink, orange and lilac 10cm/4in squares of each)
* Scrap white card
* 1 x Woodware Super Duper lever flower punch
* 1 x Woodware Large lever circle punch
* PVA glue
* Glue spreader
* Roller glue pen
* Scissors
* Ruler
* Pencil
* Embossing tool

GLITTER:
* Self-adhesive vinyl
* Iridescent white glitter

Glitter 101+

Frost the edges of a real bunch of flowers with a little paste made of icing sugar to act as a glue, and sprinkle with edible glitter. The effect looks particularly magnificent on rose petals.

MAKE IT:

1 Punch six flowers; one each from the pink, pale orange and lilac card and three more from the self-adhesive vinyl. Peel off the backing and stick a glittered vinyl flower to each of the card flowers.

2 Punch three circles from white card, cover with PVA glue and sprinkle with iridescent white glitter. Allow to dry, then glue a glittered circle in the centre of each flower.

3 Fold the purple paper in half. With the folded edge nearest you, draw two 2.2cm/1in vertical lines, 5cm/2in in from each edge. Join with a horizontal line. Cut the two vertical lines with scissors and use the embossing tool to score along the horizontal line. Flip over and repeat the embossed line on the other side.

4 Open up the paper and fold again, this time pushing forward the cut section to form a step.

5 Insert the purple sheet inside the card and glue it in place, ensuring the edges join up.

6 Lay the three flowers in a row with the middle flower in front overlapping both the left hand and right hand flowers. Glue them to each other.

7 Open the card and lay the row of flowers face down on the bottom of the card as near to the bottom of the step as you can. Fold the top of the card down to check where the step will touch against the flowers. Dot PVA glue on the part of the flowers that will touch the step, fold the top of the card down and allow to dry. Take care not to put glue anywhere that it may cause the two halves of the card to stick together.

WITH THIS RING...

Card making does not need to take all afternoon. These speedy wedding cards can be whipped up in five minutes and are perfect for invitations, to announce your engagement or even to hand over as you drop down on one knee.

CRAFT STASH:
* Thin card
* Card (cream)
* Scissors
* Ruler
* Pencil

GLITTER:
* Self-adhesive vinyl

Template page 205

MAKE IT:

1. Fold your card and cut into a square that measures 15x15cm/ 6x6in.

2. Cut a square of vinyl for the background (blue) just smaller than the main card (approx 2mm/.1in), peel off the backing and smooth onto the base card using a ruler to push out any air bubbles.

3. Copy the template onto thin card and cut out the ring shape by cutting the jewel off the ring base.

4. Draw around the base on gold vinyl, cut it out, peel off the backing and smooth it into place. Repeat this with the jewel on white vinyl.

5. Cut strips of silver vinyl that measure 0.5 cm/.2in. Hold these against the edges of the jewel, trim them to size and stick them on. Add the strips inside the jewel to add definition.

Glitter 101+

Pour glitter into card cones along with dried flower buds and heart shaped sequins to make extra special wedding confetti.

TOP TIP:
You can use this template to make the design from glittery card but vinyl is much quicker! There is no need to worry about gluing things down, it's flat, very sticky and creates a fabulous glossy effect.

185

PRECIOUS MEMORIES

I'm one of those people who is guilty of taking vast quantities of digital photos and leaving them on my computer to gather virtual dust. Some photos are far more special than others and these deserve better treatment. Scrapbooking is a craft that is all about showing off and celebrating your favourite photographs and it beats having them hidden away inside an album. Give it a go and be as experimental as you like.

Designed by Jennifer Grace

CRAFT STASH:

* A photograph approx 15x10cm/ 6x4in
* Patterned paper
* White gel pen
* Round flat buttons 1.7cm/.7in diameter (3)
* Roller glue pen
* PVA glue
* Craft dots
* Craft knife and ruler
* Papermania 3D petals template (optional)

GLITTER:

* Fine
* Sparkly paper (pink and blue)
* Letters
* Sparkly pen

MAKE IT:

1. Dip the buttons flat side up into PVA glue, then place two of them in a small pile of blue glitter, and one in pink. Pat down with your fingertips and leave to dry.

2. Cut a 30cm/ 12in square of blue paper using a craft knife, this is the backing sheet. Then cut a 27cm/10.5in one from your first patterned paper – glue this on to the centre of the blue.

3. Mount your photo on to the pink paper using the adhesive roller, then cut this down leaving a 1.1cm/.4in pink border around your photo.

4. Cut a 4cm/1.6in wide strip off your second patterned paper. Cut it down to 20x3cm/ 8x1.2in . Adhere your title words using the black and white glitter alphabet stickers to the pink side of the paper.

5. Cut a 9.5x8cm/ 4x3in rectangle from the blue paper scraps. On the matt side doodle a scalloped border using the white gel pen, and write your information using the black sparkle pen and affix.

6. Stick the mounted photo onto your page, overlapping the information block slightly and glue the title strip above.

7. Use the 3D petal template to cut five flowers from your scraps of papers, or cut out your own, and then layer them so you have three flowers in total. Stick your glittery buttons into the centres using glue dots, and stick them onto your page in the same way.

8. Use your glue pen to draw swirls onto your paper and sprinkle with pink glitter. Leave to dry, shake off the excess, and then draw more swirls and repeat with blue glitter.

TOP TIP:

When dipping the buttons into the PVA and glitter, stick a blob of blue tack to the back to help you hold it.

TOP TIP:
If you find it hard to write in a straight line on plain paper you can draw pencil lines using a ruler then erase them once the ink is dry.

LITTLE LADY

My baby girl is starting to look so grown up, especially when she's 'modelling' a cute hat! She's such a sweet, pretty, (sometimes bossy) little lady!!

Glitter 101+

Make embellishments for scrap-booking. Use a craft punch to create shapes like hearts and stars, coat them in PVA glue, then press on the glitter. When dry, use them in all your paper-craft projects.

PIN UP GIRL

Bling is my thing. I've jewel encrusted my computer, camera, sewing machine, iron and various garments. One day, I aspire to dazzle up all my pictures too; turning ordinary poster prints into works of art. OK, so diamante glitz is not to everyone's taste, but a single sparkling picture against a plain wall can have incredible, mood enhancing effects. Watch it under different lights and be amazed at how the gemstones catch sunrays, shimmer by lamplight and put a smile on surprised guests.

CRAFT STASH:
* A poster of your choice
* Acrylic gemstones
* PVA glue
* Fine tip applicator or toothpick
* Tweezers
* Collage materials (sequins/ plastic flowers) (optional)

GLITTER:
* Glitter glues
* Glitter glue paint

MAKE IT:

Highlight aspects of the image by applying glue using a fine tip applicator and sprinkling glitter on top. You can cover whole areas of the design or just embellish details. To affix the gemstones lift them up using tweezers and stick on any other collage items you like.

TOP TIP:
For a truly special project, swap acrylic gemstones for Swarovski crystals. Warning: it will be expensive but with their incredible diamond shimmer, and vivid hues, the end result will be spectacular.

Glitter 101+

Want to make your own hula garland? Thread glitter glue coated plastic flowers onto a long piece of thread, tie the end and wear around your neck.

SURPRISE! SURPRISE!

Personalise your presents with hand printed wrapping paper. Your friends will be so impressed they won't want to open your gift, so it doesn't matter what is inside!

Designed by Jennifer Grace

CRAFT STASH:

* Roll of brown paper approx 70cm/27.5in tall
* Acrylic paint (purple and iridescent white)
* Fiskars shape template Doodles
* Masking tape
* Paintbrush
* Roller glue pen

GLITTER:

* White glitter paint
* Fine

MAKE IT:

1. Cut a sheet of brown paper from the roll approximately 58cm/23in wide. Lay it down on a protective surface to paint on.

2. Use masking tape to cover any bits of the template where you are worried you might paint through the wrong hole. Tape the front and the back of the template so there are no tacky bits left showing that might stick to the brown paper.

3. Mix the purple and white acrylic, and the glitter paint together until you have the shade you want. Do not add too much glitter paint or the consistency will be too thin, one third at most.

4. Paint through the template holes using a stippling motion (tapping the tip of the brush rather than using brushstrokes). Keep moving the template and repeating until you have filled the sheet of paper and leave to dry.

5. Use the roller glue pen to draw a swirl onto the paper, then tip on some fine glitter. Keep repeating in various places until you are pleased with the distribution of sparkle.

6. When dry carefully tip off the excess glitter onto a folded sheet of paper to collect it back up. To finish brush off any unwanted speckles of glitter using a soft paintbrush or blusher brush.

Glitter 101+

Make a glittery masterpiece Jackson Pollack style. Lay out a large sheet of paper or canvas. Dip your brushes into glitter paint and flick, flick, flick! You will end up with an abstract work of art.

TOP TIP: For a children's project use foam stamps or sponges instead of the stencil.

TEMPLATES & RESOURCES

TRANSFERRING IMAGES

Some of the projects in this book come with templates so that you can use the same images and motifs in your own glitter crafting. First of all you will need to photocopy them. Increase the template to the size you require. Your local copy shop can help you adjust the settings so you end up with the right dimensions.

How to use templates
Cut your photocopied image out, glue onto thin card, and cut out again. This shape can then be drawn around as required.

How to use transfer paper/carbon paper
Place your transfer paper/carbon paper on top of the surface you want the image to be on. Place the photocopied image on top of that. Secure with masking tape along the edges to ensure the image does not move. Use a pencil to draw over this image. These marks will transfer through the carbon paper and onto the surface of your choice. If the lines are too faint, you can go over them using a pen or pencil.

BE THE EYE OF THE TIGER...

See page 64

THE TABLE IS SET
See page 180

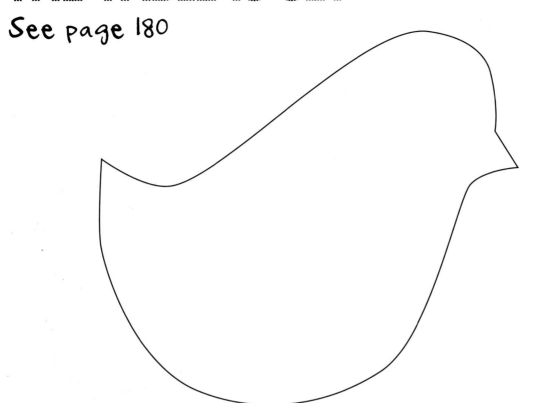

BIRDS OF PARADISE
See page 156

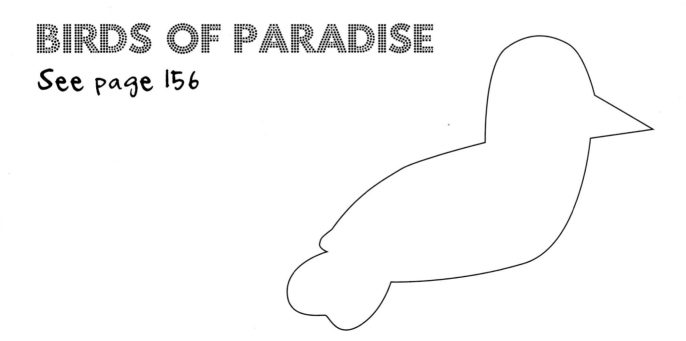

TREE OF LIFE

See page 72

CROWNING GLORY

See page 165

SHOE STOPPER

See page 32

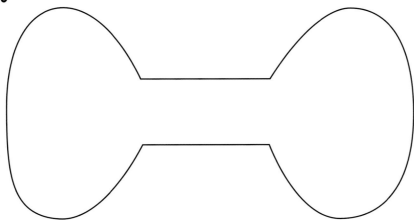

THIS HOLLYWOOD LIFE

See page 51 and also use for page 160

SHAKE IT UP!

See page 118

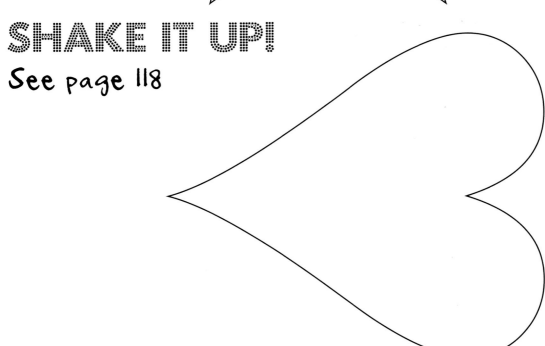

BABY GA GA

See page 170

'WHY DOES IT ALWAYS RAIN ON ME?'

See page 59

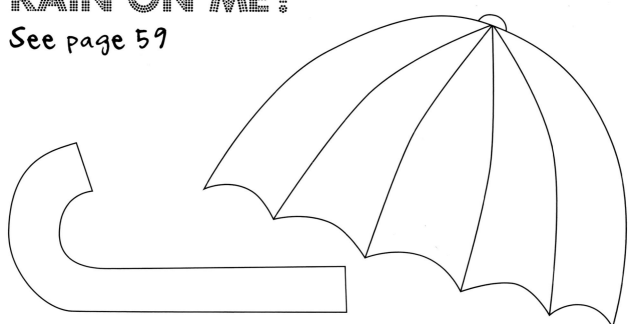

TRAVEL BUG

See page 169

WINGS OF DESIRE

See page 162

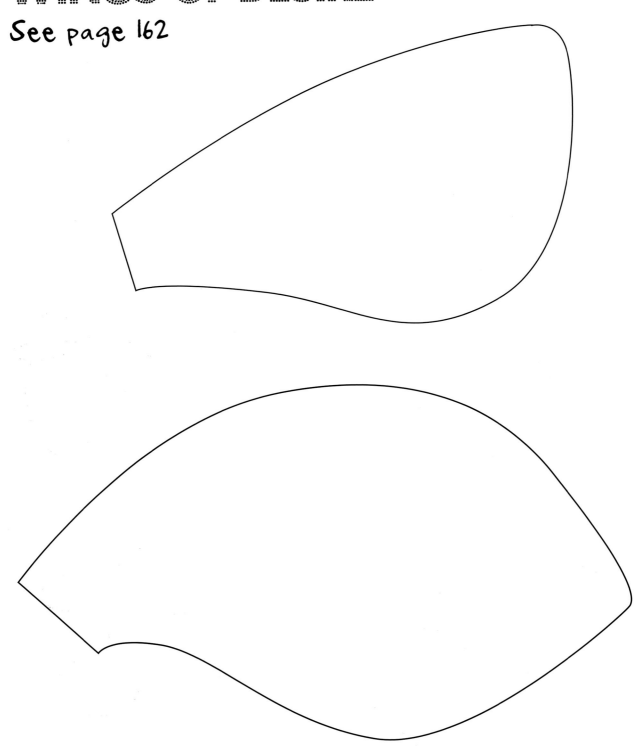

FEELING FRUITY

See page 163

SHE WAS A SHOWGIRL...

See page 50

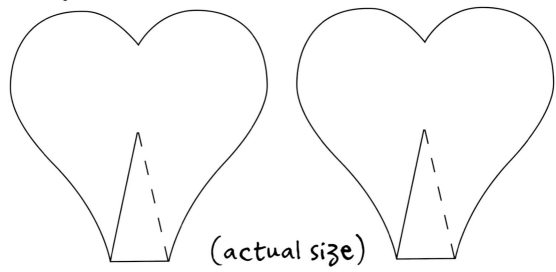

(actual size)

HERE COME THE GIRLS

See page 132

WITH THIS RING...

See page 185

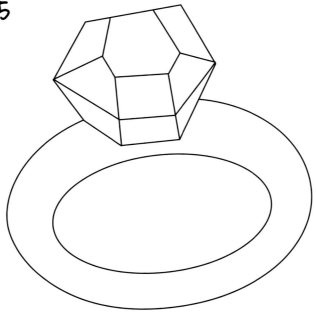

HORNY DEVIL

See page 36

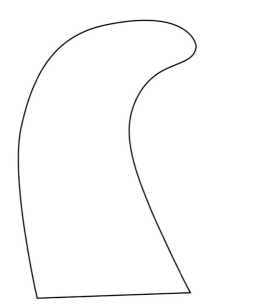
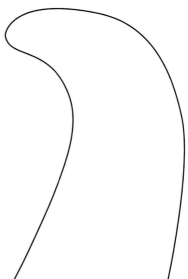

GLOBAL GATHERING

See page 178

ALL STOCKED UP

See page 148

SHAKEN, NOT STIRRED...
See page 84

SEASONAL SNOWFLAKES

See page 100

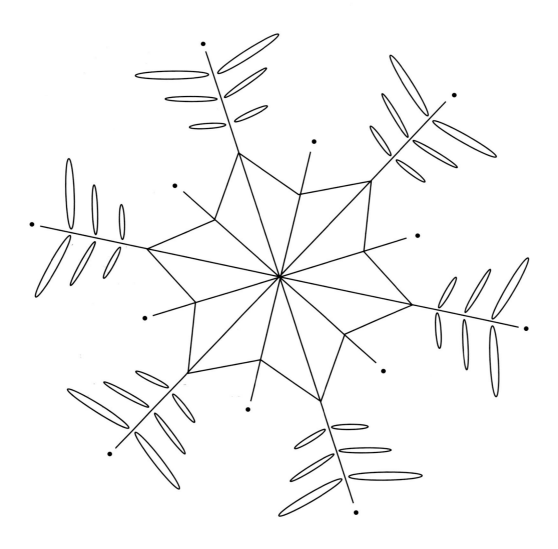

- French knot

⬭ Detached chain (lazy daisy) stitch

THE CASE IS CLOSED!

See page 144

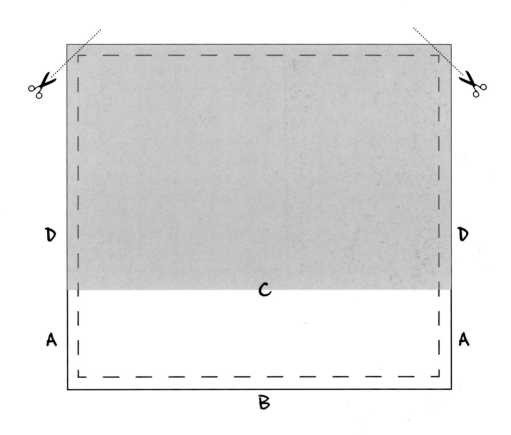

D   D

C

A   A

B

Key

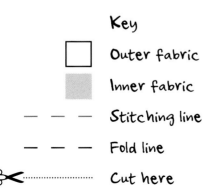

Outer fabric

Inner fabric

Stitching line

Fold line

Cut here

WHERE TO SHOP

The materials to make these projects were sourced from the shops and online stores listed below. Most of them will ship internationally, but remember you don't need to find the exact items. Visit local craft shops and haberdasheries near you to see what similar fabrics and glitters you can find. An excellent place to source craft materials is from auction website eBay (www.ebay.com) so if there are any you are having difficulty tracking down, try there. Also see what you already own that you can re-use and don't forget to ask friends and family if they have any materials they can share.

Glitter

Art Glitter www.artglitter.com
Brian Clegg www.brianclegg.co.uk
Candle www.fullmoons-cauldron.co.uk
Confetti glue www.hobbycraft.co.uk
Crafty Chica www.ilovetocreate.com
Craft glitter www.craftglitter.co.uk
DecoArt www.decoart.com
Edible www.edible-glitter.co.uk
Fabric www.josyrose.com
German glass www.stampeezee.co.uk
Pebeo Touch www.paperchase.co.uk
Plasti-Kote spray www.hobbycraft.co.uk
Rainbow Turtle www.rainbowturtle.com
Rangers Stickles glitter and glues
www.glitterpot.co.uk
Veiling www.thetrimmingcompany.com
Vinyl www.craftcreations.com

General materials

Acrylic gems
www.creativebeadcraft.co.uk
Baker's Twine www.ribbongirl.co.uk
Double-sided tack mounting film
www.hobbycraft.co.uk
Embroidery floss (Anchor)
www.coatscrafts.co.uk
Felt www.lupinhandmade.com
Fine Tip Applicator www.finetip.co.uk
Gelly pens www.sakuraofamerica.com
Jewellery findings
www.londonbeadco.co.uk
Swarovski crystals
www.creativebeadcraft.co.uk

Specialist craft materials

American Crafts Zing embossing powder
www.sarahscardsltd.com
Cosmic Shimmer embossing powder
www.countryviewcrafts.co.uk
Galeria Mineral texture gel
www.hobbycraft.co.uk
Glass Paint www.paintforglass.co.uk
Heat It Up! embossing powders
www.countryviewcrafts.co.uk
Hot Spots! www.nid-noi.com
Lazertran www.lazertran.com
Moon Glow embossing powders
www.lindystampgang.com
Scrapbooking supplies
www.twopeasinabucket.com
Shephards Falkiners bookmaking
supplies www.falkiners.com
Siligum Moulding paste
www.homecrafts.co.uk
Stampendous embossing powder
www.craftobsessions.co.uk
Stamp pads www.tsukineko.com
Vanilla Paste www.littlepod.co.uk
Versamark Watermark stamp pad
www.craftathome.co.uk

Project items

Blank tote bags
www.cleverbaggers.co.uk
Candle wax, scent, wicks and colour
www.fullmoons-cauldron.co.uk
Comics www.forbiddenplanet.com
www.orbitalcomics.com

Clock mechanism and handles
www.clockparts.co.uk
Glass cut to size
www.glassinlondon.co.uk
Debrina Pratt decoupage sheets
www.etsy.com/shop/
landofenchantment
Millinery supplies
www.tiaramaking.com
www.macculloch-wallis.co.uk
Maya Road Cat keychain set
www.craftathome.co.uk
Penny Black 'Tree scene' stamp
www.hobbyartstamps.com
www.pennyblackinc.com
Resin & mould www.metalclay.co.uk
Roly Poly Votive Holder
www.homearomas.co.uk
Spa crafting www.bathbomb.biz
Shrinkles Paper www.hobbycraft.co.uk
Scrapbooking www.papermaze.co.uk
www.therange.co.uk

Craft stores

A. C. Moore www.acmoore.com
Craft Superstore
www.craftsuperstore.co.uk
Hobby Craft www.hobbycraft.co.uk
Jo-Ann Stores www.joann.com
Loisirs et Création
www.loisirsetcreation.com
Michaels Stores "Where Creativity
Happens" www.michaels.com
Riots Stores "For Creative Hearts"
www.riotstores.com.au

FEATURED STOCKISTS

Craft Creations

Are specialists in papercrafts, stocking greeting card blanks, decoupage sheets and stickers. They supply adhesive vinyl and card glitter, Tulip glitter tube paints and outline stickers.
www.craftcreations.com

Fred Aldous Limited

A family run crafts business spanning over five generations and 125 years, the company sells all general craft supplies and a huge range of glitters including their own brand, iron-on glitter, sprays and Glitz It glues.
www.fredaldous.co.uk

Hobbycraft

The biggest art and craft store in the UK, there are over 60 branches based in large retail outlets. They sell craft materials for all types of crafting including stamping, sewing, knitting and painting and supply their own brand of glitters and glues as well as high-end brands like Martha Stewart.
www.hobbycraft.co.uk

Fine Tip Applicator

Is a precision tool that applies PVA glues in fine lines (.5mm) enabling you to create extremely detailed glitter patterns.
www.finetip.co.uk

Josy Rose

Is a modern online haberdashery specialising in high fashion craft materials from feathers and facemasks to corsetry and jewellery making supplies. They also sell richly glittered fabrics and unique shades of loose glitter.
www.josyrose.com

CONTRIBUTORS
MEET THE GLITTER EXPERTS:

Brittany De Staedtler
(bath bombs)
Is the owner and founder of Posh Brats Bath & Body Boutique, who specialise in handmade, natural toiletries. Originally hailing from Mississippi, USA, Brittany now lives in the UK and her workshop is based in Cheshire.
(www.poshbrats.com)

Emily Burt
(place cards)
Emily is a young designer-maker and writer. She and her partner own Shipshape Studio, a craft venue and shop in Northwood, Greater London, where you can learn to make craft projects, or hire out the venue for a celebration.
(www.handmadebyemily.com)

Caz Turner
(pompom jewellery)
Caz's fondest memories of being a child are growing up in Australia and hearing the click of her mother's knitting needles. She is mainly a sewer and is currently teaching herself crochet and knitting. Caz lives in Singapore.
(www.usefulbox.blogspot.com)

Emma Watson
(hanger)
An experimental crafter with a keen interest in trying new techniques. She also sells her work at markets and teaches crafts.
(pumpsville@hotmail.co.uk)

Claire Barone
(plate)
A fine artist and painter who enjoys experimenting with collage and mixed media.
(www.clairebarone.com)

Fatema Hossain
(paper beads)
Is a scientist turned artist who began life as a microbiologist before training as a lifecoach then turning her hand to the more creative discipline of art and design.
(www.etsy.com/shop/LittleRaraAvis)

Elisa Begg
(clock)
Runs an online handmade gift shop based in the far north of Scotland specialising in personalised items.
(www.elibeegifts.co.uk)

Gemma Andrews
(pendant)
A self-taught experimental jewellery maker and maths tutor.
(www.damselflygemma.co.uk)

Gemma Corner

(key ring)

Has been crafting since she was small and regards making things as an extension of her personality. (www.booteeq.etsy.com)

Hatastic!

(fascinator)

Was founded in 2009 by Chloë Haywood who has been nominated for an Accessory Designer of the Year award. Her hats have been featured in major publications including *The Times*, *OK Magazine* and *Cosmopolitan*. (www.hatastic.co.uk)

Helen Hammond

(lipgloss)

An aromatherapist and the owner of Scents-ible Solutions who produce handmade natural skin care, health & wellbeing and spa products. All their ingredients are ethically sourced, fair trade and are never tested upon animals, they use pure essential oils, plant extracts and botanicals. (www.scentsiblesolutions.co.uk)

Jennifer Grace

(scrapbook)

A crafting addict from Dorset, and self-employed Creative Writing, Art, and Craft tutor. (www.jennifersjumbles.blogspot.com)

Jolekha Shasha

(cookies)

Is an HR professional and amateur sports photographer who loves to spend her spare time rustling up cakes and sweet treats. (jolekha@hotmail.com)

Kathy Cano-Murillo

(duck)

AKA The Crafty Chica, an Arizona based craft celebrity. She is the author of several crafts books and has most recently been writing craft fiction, selling her own brand products and presenting craft TV. (www.craftychica.com)

Kirsty Neale

(xmas decorations)

A freelance writer and designer-maker. Her work has been published in numerous magazines, including Papercraft Inspirations and Mollie Makes. (www.kirstyneale.typepad.com)

Louise Bird

(umbrella bag)

Grew up in South Africa and became fascinated with cloth after spending several years working in clothing manufacturing. She now uses her passion for fabric for creating and selling handmade gifts and textiles. (www.folksy.com/shops/loopyloo)

CONTRIBUTORS
MEET THE GLITTER EXPERTS:

Manju Malhi
(jam)
Is a well known British Indian chef known for offering western cuisine to India and Indian cooking to the western world through her books, TV shows, cooking demonstrations and charity work with organisations such as the VSO. She writes about cooking, healthy eating and using spices for international publications.
(www.manjumalhi.com)

Raye McKown
(bunting)
Designs and sells handmade jewellery, knitted and crocheted accessories under her label Aurora Bloom and teaches crafts to local community groups.
(www.aurorabloom.co.uk)

Rebecca Holder
(gel candle)
Runs The Handmade Emporium, Oundle, selling and creating handmade crafts. She loves to paint glass and create gel wax candles.
(www.thehandmadeemporium.com)

Ruth Crean
(earrings)
Is an Irish designer living and working in Limerick City. After graduating with a degree in Fine Art: Printmaking, she has worked in many different disciplines including painting, photography, digital art, graphic design, paper crafts, theatre design and fashion. In 2007 she set up Nice Day Designs selling handcrafts and accessories.
(www.nicedaydesigns.org)

Shimelle Laine
(tape)
A London-based American crafter who spends most of her hours scrapbooking. She blogs and teaches online craft classes.
(www.shimelle.com)

Talulah Blue
(nipple tassels)
Is a costumier and burlesque performer.
(www.talulahblue.com)

Virginia Fox
(Xmas card)
Trained in Calligraphy, Heraldry and Illumination at Reigate School of Art, she is now a corporate designer at a large consultancy firm in London. In her spare time she makes and sells cards.
(virginia.fox@virgin.net)

Venus Muscat
(wings)
Originally from Scarborough, Venus now lives in Manchester with her two girls and cat. She spends weekends at her allotment or camping and has been making fairy/butterfly wings for children and adults since 2004.
(www.etsy.com/shop/venuscreations)

ABOUT THE AUTHOR

MOMTAZ BEGUM-HOSSAIN

To say I like making things is an understatement; even my blog is called CosILikeMakingStuff. blogspot.com. The fascination began when I was a child. I used to chop up egg cartons and find new uses for them and I am pleased to say, this very modest of materials is still in my craft stash. In fact, an 'egg tray' makes an appearance in this very book.

Inspiration strikes me every single day, most commonly from people I observe wandering the streets of London. It's a capital city brimming with life, colour, culture and creativity. From discovering random acts of guerrilla knitting on lamp posts to being able to watch vibrant Bollywood movies at my local cinema and wandering markets filled with African print fabrics; all around are beautiful images that fuel the senses and imagination. It's a crafter's paradise and as long as I am surrounded by such visions, I will continue to create.

www.momtazbh.co.uk
Twitter: TheCraftCafe

Photo: Alexandre Pichon

ACKNOWLEDGEMENTS

Further reading:

Glitter: A Brief History by Aja Mangum
New York Magazine (2007)

Glitter Artistry by Barbara Trombley
(Published by A Lark/Chapelle Books) 2008

Waking up in the Land of Glitter by Kathy Cano-Murillo
(Hachette Book Group) 2010

Projects:

Bow tie project is adapted from 'How To Sew a Bow Tie'
on AllFreeSewing.com.

Kitchen tins, the 'Treat Tin' originally appeared in the
November 2011 issue of Dog's Monthly magazine, published
by ABM Publishing, designed by Momtaz Begum-Hossain

Bolster design is inspired by the sci-fi Bollywood bolster that
appears in 'Bollywood Crafts: 20 Projects inspired by Popular
Indian Cinema by Momtaz Begum-Hossain, published by
GMC Publications, 2006.

Christmas stocking based on a design that appeared in the
December 2011 issue of Dog's Monthly magazine, published
by ABM Publishing, designed by Momtaz Begum-Hossain

Newspaper nails adapted from an idea published
on the Topshop blog
http://insideout.topshop.com, July 2011

Glitter:

Many thanks to the following companies who provided
glitter to make some of the projects featured in the book;
Craft Creations, Fred Aldous, Hobbycraft and Josy Rose,
and to Anne Peak who designed and supplied the Fine Tip
Applicator that was used throughout.

Model:

Special thanks to actress and comedian Nadia Kamil
for starring in the fashion & accessories section.
(www.nadiakamil.co.uk)

Personal note:

Thank you to the team at Vivays Publishing, Roger from
Struktur Design for letting me take over his photography
studio with glitter and all the contributors who designed
projects for the book. Extra special thanks to Kathy Cano-
Murillo, who is my craft heroine, the online craft community
whose enthusiasm and positive spirit helped me keep on track,
Taylor Coburn from RJA Plastics for providing a unique behind
the scenes insight into their glitter factory, based in Germany,
make-up artist Annie Shah and the team at *Asiana* magazine.

This book is dedicated to my three sisters, Fatema, Jahura
and Jolekha who have all contributed to it in some way, and
whose encouragement and motivation knows no bounds,
and to Ponting who always makes me laugh.